#NOW

Dr. Max McKeown

author of *The Strategy Book*

#NOW

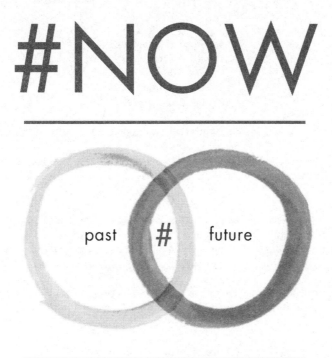

past # future

The Surprising Truth
About the Power of Now

Aurum
Press

Quarto is the authority on a wide range of topics.

Quarto educates, entertains and enriches the lives of
our readers—enthusiasts and lovers of hands-on living.

www.QuartoKnows.com

First published in Great Britain
2016 by Aurum Press Ltd
74–77 White Lion Street
Islington
London N1 9PF

A catalogue record for this book is
available from the British Library.

ISBN 978 1 78131 518 7
Ebook ISBN 978 1 78131 634 4

1 3 5 7 9 10 8 6 4 2
2016 2018 2020 2019 2017

Typeset in Berkeley by SX Composing DTP, Rayleigh, Essex
Printed by CPI Group (UK) Ltd, Croydon CR0 4YY

For my children, Brontë, Zak, Steiny, and Reuben.
Each one beautiful, talented, and not finished yet.

CONTENTS

LET'S START WITH #NOW

Now is an exciting and demanding place to be, unavoidable and unmissable. The present moment is everything and nothing. One billion moments in a lifetime. Nowists don't hide in the #Now. Instead, they use power from the past, present and future to tip them towards positive action. They don't want to slow down, so they nurture their nowness.

PART ONE

NURTURING YOUR NOWNESS

YOUR NEED FOR SPEED

Making incredibly fast decisions is often looked on as impulsive, and being impulsive is often seen as bad. But what if, Dickman asked, there was a different kind of impulsive? And what if, Kruglanski echoed, some people have learned to take action and decide faster because they just love that sense of purpose that comes from moving at speed?

KEEP YOUR #NOW MOVING

Wanting to keep moving is a deeply powerful motivation. If what moves us to movement is the desire to move, we never want to stop. We want to do what is in front of us. We want to go with what feels right. And when we feel this way, our ultimate reward is the thrill of effortless action.

PART TWO

THE THREE STREAMS OF #NOW

CONTENTS

Nowists embrace the richness of life, and reject over-focus. They believe in more than one priority, and are passionate about more than one big idea, project, profession and pastime. They move between multiple streams of #Now so they can remember without being overwhelmed, and strategically move between streams of action.

PART THREE

THE #NOWIST TOOLKIT

INTRODUCTION
LET'S START WITH #NOW

All we've got is #Now. Life, composed of a billion moments, from our first to our last thoughts. Some voices tell us to slow down, yet our human nature urges us all to move forward.[1]

Some people resist this evolutionary momentum. They listen to the voice that tells them to slow down and develop habits to keep them from going anywhere new or better. They may push back against the natural flux of sensations – labelling them interruptions or irritations – and so waste the spontaneous energy of life lived effortlessly.

This book argues that for most people, most of the time, it is better to lean towards action rather than

THIS IS

#NOW

past # future

inaction. Nowists act on their belief that they will be happier and healthier if they keep moving. That they will achieve more and experience more if they move forward than if they stand still. The virtue of impatience is often of greater practical use than the vice of self-denying, motion-delaying, joy-draining, now-numbing patience.

The circles on the cover – and on the previous pages – represent time and our perception of time, with the present at the intersection of past and future. The # represents Now. It is the point at which life is experienced and action can be taken or not taken. It is here that everything you do is done. And it is when everything you will ever make happen first happens.

Your #Now can be happy and connected. Or unhappy, disconnected and overwhelmed. Your #Now can be bored or captivated, scared or fearless, joyful or joyless. Nowists get off on getting on, so they run when they could walk, jump when they could sit, and dance when they could sit at the edge. They regret inaction, so simply act.

This is a book about the joy of moving. It is a book about motivation, because motivation means to *be moved*. This is also a book about what it takes to keep moving – ways of making the effortless decisions required to clear a path for clear effortless action – and the benefits this brings for your sense of power and well-being.

It explores surprising discoveries that reveal powerful truths about how we use our individual #Now. How easily we can slip into a passive *Thenist* state – where our time is spent comparing ourselves with others, regretting what could have been, complaining about what is, and fearing what might never happen. If we're too careful, we can end up with a thousand different action plans that block taking *any* action, and leave us worrying rather than loving life.

To accurately describe the alternative, a *Nowist* approach, we're going to learn more about functional impulsivity, and the locomotion mindset. And then we're going to reveal more threads, including the ability to see patterns at speed, the ability to use mental time travel effectively, and the ability to take mental shortcuts to action. Taken together we're going to discuss the kind of behaviours that effectively harness the power and joy of #Now.

what you can't change

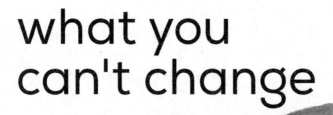

past

where everytl

what you can change

future

ng changes

PART ONE
NURTURING YOUR NOWNESS

CHAPTER 1
YOUR NEED FOR SPEED

In the last couple of decades of the twentieth century, with the Soviet Union collapsing, the Internet getting started, and hip hop going worldwide, two curious scientists ran some experiments that produced some very surprising implications for the twenty-first century.

The first of these was Scott J. Dickman, a doctoral student working in the Brain, Cognition, and Action Laboratory at the University of Michigan.

One month in 1985, Dickman carried out a series of three experiments. Before the experiments started, the participants took a standard test for the personality trait of impulsivity. Each person then sat down at a table with a deck of thirty-six cards in front of them. The cards, which were about the size of a smartphone, were each emblazoned with a large letter made up of smaller letters. On the command 'Ready, set, go!' the participants completed three variations of the task: sorting the cards into piles based on the large letter, the small letters, or a mixture of both.[2] The groups were asked to sort the cards as quickly and accurately as possible. Dickman expected the experiment to show that highly impulsive people would find it more difficult to complete the tasks. They would lack focus, struggle to ignore distractions, or fail to bring different information together. This was his expectation because that was the traditional view of both society *and* psychology. Impulsivity was seen as dysfunctional.

To his great surprise, people with high impulsivity scored as highly on the card-sorting tests as people with low impulsivity. Dickman couldn't explain his results, so he ran another set of experiments to try and figure out what was really going on.

This time he included colour as a third piece of information, to make the task harder and really emphasise the processing differences between high and low impulsives. People had to sort cards based on the big letter, the small letter and the colour. All groups had to combine relevant information, and ignore irrelevant information. Once again, the high impulsives did just as well as the low impulsives.

The mystery had deepened, and so had the value of solving it. To answer the question, Dickman proposed an original idea – that some of the high impulsives used different strategies to low impulsives. They choose speed over accuracy, and, in this particular test, speed over accuracy led to results that matched those scored by low impulsives, who privileged accuracy over speed.

Highly impulsive individuals value rapid responses, he said, in part because they were willing to make and correct errors. Less impulsive people are more concerned with avoiding mistakes, so take more time to decide and act, even when any errors are easy to correct.

Intrigued, Dickman, devised new experiments to find out more about when high impulsivity gave people an advantage. Participants looked at pairs of geometric shapes, and had to decide whether they were the same or different. When speed was rewarded more than accuracy, or participants were put under time pressure, the high impulsives did best.

The breakthrough came when Dickman asked an insightful question. 'Could it be', he said, 'that there are two separate traits?' The kind that pushes people to decide quickly in a way that is likely to lead to bad consequences. And the kind that allows people to decide quickly with good results.[3]

This wasn't just another way of saying high and low impulsivity. He had found two distinct behavioural traits. The traditional kind was dysfunctional impulsivity. Under pressure, people lurch into actions or decisions, without adequate understanding. Sometimes this may work out, but more often it does not.

'It would be an awful waste of talent and potential if people assumed that slow thinking is always better thinking.'

Other people benefit from functional impulsivity. They appear to spend less time thinking about what they do before they do it, but this is because they are particularly good at deciding fast. They think clearly under pressure. They see options rapidly, and prefer to do more, even at the cost of making more mistakes.

Dickman carefully constructed a series of twenty-three questions – a scale that distinguished between functional and dysfunctional impulsivity. He then repeated some of his earlier experiments, and found that much of the time functional impulsivity explained high performance at high speed. Dysfunctional impulsives were fast, but so inaccurate that their advantage often disappeared.

Since Dickman's pioneering work and surprising discoveries, other scientists have identified situations in which functional impulsivity can be valuable.

YOU GET TOLD TO
LOOK BEFORE YOU
LEAP
BUT IF YOU
ARE TOO
CAREFUL
YOU MAY END UP
JUST
LOOKING

People who are highly functionally impulsive can deal with the now with such speed and clarity that they have an advantage. It would be an awful waste of talent and potential if people assumed that slow thinking is always better thinking.

The next stop in our story about the surprising truth about the power of #Now is the University of Maryland. Here, one of the greatest living psychologists, Arie Kruglanski, turned his attention to the difference between two kinds of guiding behaviour.[4]

Imagine, he asked, two people driving together to the supermarket. One wants to find the perfect parking spot, even if this means delaying the moment when they can start shopping. The other wants to park in the first available place, even at the price of a longer walk from their parking space to the store.[5]

The first person is guided by what Kruglanski called assessment. When people think like this, he wondered, maybe they focus on figuring out the perfect choice rather than getting anything done.

Their companion is guided by what Kruglanski called locomotion. When people think like this, he mused, perhaps they just want to get on with doing, rather than worrying about getting the decision absolutely right.

It seemed to make sense, and it passed the common experience test: we have all felt the pleasure of moving on, and we have all felt the pain of indecision. But, as a scientist, Kruglanski wanted to discover more about the differences between people with these two mindsets, and how these differences impacted on their health, happiness, accomplishment and life satisfaction.

With the help of graduate students and long-time collaborators, Higgins and Kruglanski came up with a list of questions that people could ask themselves to indicate where they were on the scale of locomotion and assessment thinking. Next they tested them on 2,500 graduate students from three universities to make sure their personality tests were reliable.

Then the team checked whether assessment and locomotion were different behaviours. They were. Results showed that high locomotors tended to be committed to action; that they can stay focused on a task and are energetic, conscientious and goal-oriented. By contrast, high assessors had a tendency to worry too much – about doing the wrong thing, any kind of ambiguity, what other people think, and how they measure up to other people. Locomotors moved. Assessors worried.

People high on assessment were anxious to prove that they were good at what they did, while locomotors enjoyed *becoming* better at what they were doing. The future was something positive for people in locomotion mode, it made them happy because it pushed them on to greater efforts in the day. But for people in assessment mode, the future is just one more thing to worry about.

The decision-making processes of those in locomotion mode weren't slowed up by unhelpful concerns about who was watching, or what might go wrong, or finding the impossibly perfect answer. People in high assessment mode made slower decisions because they couldn't let go. This burden of indecision made life *feel* less enjoyable. They did not sit back and relax, they worked and worried.

Surprisingly, they found that assessment and locomotion modes are not opposites. You can be high in one, or neither, or both. This means that people may love moving on but be sabotaged by their need for a perfect answer, or fear of failure. Equally, someone may not worry about what others think, but that does not mean that they necessarily want to get anything done. We'll return to the practical importance of this discovery in the next chapter and throughout this book.

After years of work, and several thousand tests, Kruglanski and his team were confident that locomotion and assessment modes showed real differences between people. They were curious to find out if those personality differences offered any advantages in the real world. Never afraid of hard work, the group designed a further four studies that predicted the impact of locomotion and assessment modes on performance. If their predictions were accurate, then their theory would have power both in the laboratory *and* in the real world.

Remember the students who took the tests designed to develop the locomotion and assessment scales? Researchers compared the academic performance of 600 of these students with their scores on locomotion and assessment personality tests taken the year before. And they found that students who were higher on the locomotion *and* assessment scales had performed best in the previous three, five and seven semesters. These students compared options *and* then worked hard to make their plans work. This was not stress, it was forward motion.

Something similar was found when researchers looked at people applying to get into an elite unit of the US army. This was a pretty brutal challenge, even for experienced soldiers. Sixty per cent of the applicants either quit or were removed before the end. Soldiers who were high on locomotion were much more likely to succeed, but only when they also scored at least moderately on assessment mode.

'High performers need to look and leap, leap and look.'

Both mindsets were necessary to turn high locomotors into high performers. High performers need to look and leap, leap and look.

This was backed up by the results of a further study Kruglanski and his colleagues pursued. They used a proofreading task in which each participant received a red pen and two booklets that they were asked to compare. Any difference found between the two booklets, or any errors, were to be circled in red. There were sixty-three genuine inconsistencies and mistakes, but those who were high on the assessment scale were trying so hard to be perfect that they ended up spotting errors that didn't actually exist.

Another experiment was designed to understand more about the way people in high locomotion mode choose goals, and how they choose to achieve them, compared to people in high assessment mode.

Participants were asked to think of five attributes they wanted to develop, then indicate how valuable each goal was to them and how difficult they thought each one would be to accomplish. They were also asked to note different approaches that they might use to achieve their aims. They were then asked to type, as fast as possible, their preferred approach. People with high locomotion scores tended to choose goals they felt confident of achieving and to quickly choose their preferred method for doing so. People with higher assessment scores did the opposite. They often picked high-value goals, even when they did not feel confident of success. They came up with lots of options for accomplishing their goals, and took a lot longer to choose their preferred method.

EFFORTLESS DECISIONS FOR EFFORTLESS ACTION

So, locomotors put themselves in a position to start quickly and finish successfully while assessors ended up stuck, sometimes even choosing more difficult tasks over more valuable ones. Yes, that's right, they somehow ignored more valuable payoffs that were easier to accomplish. Past a certain level, high assessment

appears to get in the way of clear thinking about what is most likely to lead to progress. Difficult tasks are picked simply because they are difficult.

Coming up with too many options, like some of the participants in this experiment, can cause a state of confusion that leads to something close to Dickman's dysfunctional impulsivity. When you're in assessment mode, you assume that coming up with more alternatives is a good thing: because surely thinking more has to be smarter than thinking less?

Unfortunately, if you waste time coming up with a range of unnecessary options, then you just end up having even less time to do the job. Your head is full of half-finished options that leave you feeling like you've done some work, but you don't have a sense of what to do next. Instead of a clear path to action, you've got a circular path of inaction. It's painful, slow – and *avoidable*.

Even advocates of slow thinking, such as Daniel Kahneman, winner of the Nobel Prize for Economics,[6] admit that such an approach has its downsides. He warns that 'the alternative to thinking intuitively is mental paralysis' and a 'laborious, difficult and costly world'.[7] Similarly, Walter Mischel, a careful investigator into self-control and originator of the famous Marshmallow Test, underlines how 'a life lived with too much delay of gratification can be as sad as one without enough of it'. Carl Honoré, a thoughtful evangelist for the 'slow movement', says that that he 'loves speed' and simply wants us to consider living according to 'our own inner tempo', whether slow – or fast.[8]

past # your #now
can be
disconnected

past #

ure

#

or your
#now can be
connected to
a much bigger
future

CHAPTER 2
KEEP YOUR #NOW MOVING

The good news is that we can all become a little more Nowist. Simply remembering a time when you enjoyed making good things happen is enough to get you into a Nowist mindset. You can change your approach to taking action. You can prime yourself for effortless action.

Nowists are effective self-leaders. So once you start thinking like a Nowist, you'll also find it easier to keep thinking like a Nowist.[9] You'll be better at persuading yourself to behave in ways you want to behave. You can talk yourself into feeling powerful. And this kind of self-talk will remind you to find joy in movement, until your natural response is to always keep moving forward.

BASEBALLS, MELONS, AND OPPORTUNITIES

Everything a Nowist sees, everything around them – ideas and objects, people and situations – tends to be understood in terms of how it can help keep them moving forward.[10] They are often better at seeing opportunities for action than other people. They are better at linking sequences of opportunities for action than other people. And they are particularly good at moving from seeing opportunities for action to actually using those opportunities to move forward.

When they see opportunities for action, they are primed by the opportunity to take action. Seeing a pair of running shoes makes them want to start running, and they are much more likely to go with the flow than walk past with passive regret. Noticing any kind of opportunity for movement is likely to trigger not only thoughts of enjoyable action, but motor responses – so the Nowist's heart rate increases when they see those shoes. Hands clench when they spot a badminton racket, or fingers fly when they see a keyboard or piano.

They are looking for movement and the payoff of change, so are likely to move towards whatever is most likely to make that happen. They are taking advantage of our natural need for momentum.

IF YOU DON'T START YOU'RE FINISHED

A ROOM FULL OF 'DOERS'

One experiment, carried out by a team of psychologists in New York, started by asking two groups to remember short examples of different ways they had behaved in the past.

If you were in the first group you were asked to think back to a time you acted like a 'doer', perhaps when you'd just finished one project and immediately got started on a new one, or when you could not wait to get started on something you'd decided to do. And if you were in the other group you were asked to think back to a time when you had been critical of yourself or your work; you compared yourself to other people, over-analysed your positive and negative characteristics, or criticised the work of others.[11]

You were then asked to use a particular kind of strategy to decide which brand of reading light to buy from a range of five similar reading lights. You either had to make a decision based on your assessment of every single one of the lights' features. Or you got to reach your decision much more quickly by looking at just one feature at a time, and discarding the light with the worst value on that feature.

After making your choice you were asked two questions. First, how much were you willing to pay for the reading light? And second, how happy did you feel? If you were in the Nowist group – making your choice in the most effortless way – it turns out that you were willing to pay more because you enjoyed the act of choosing, the *doing*. Enjoyment in the doing of a thing is part of the value you give to the thing. Effortless action makes the action more enjoyable. And as a Nowist you are guided by this joy.

THREE JOYS OF NOW

This is a point worth underlining, because it highlights one of the most successful and natural parts of momentum. By seeing joy in the doing of a thing, in the having done the thing, and in opportunities for doing more things, you are allowing momentum to drive you forwards to more successes. The mere act of doing creates more opportunities for doing, and leads to greater joy. This may sound simple, but without this approach the opposite is just as easy to fall into – the paralysis of inaction caused by over-assessment can mean that the best that can be experienced is the absence of disappointment.

When you are motivated by the pleasure of moving forward, you are more likely to feel good. The way you feel is directly linked to the enjoyment of action and the control that this enjoyment brings rather than the stress and anxiety that is caused by things out of your control, such as future outcomes or the judgements of others.

The way Nowists look at getting on with life has an impact on how they experience happiness, or well-being, in a couple of ways.

One way of assessing happiness is to ask yourself how you measure up to a list of beliefs that are logically thought to be important for well-being.[12] You are asked questions like: are you confident in your opinions? Do you feel in charge of situations? Do you feel new experiences are important for challenging yourself? Would other people describe you as helpful? How well do you accept yourself? Like most people, do you wander aimlessly in life?

This contrasts with another way of measuring happiness, which more straightforwardly reaches a 'score' by adding up each time you have a positive emotion and then subtracting each time you've had a negative emotion.

The checkbox approach to adding up happiness appeals to people who want external proof that they *are* happy, because their strengths or skills or attributes prove that they *are* happy. So it's an approach that is attractive to those of a more Thenist disposition, or in a more Thenist mindset. They may be happy on paper, but this does not inevitably translate into being happy in life.

Nowists find it more natural to just know whether they are happy, based on how they feel. Even when they feel less full of the joys of life, when they tally up the good and bad experiences, happiness comes out ahead. Partly because they see the upside, and partly because they do so much that is pleasurable, and take so much pleasure from what they do, their lives tend to be joy-filled.

THE CERTAIN UNCERTAINTY OF JOY

Nowists are more likely to experience joy because they embrace the uncertainty of existence. They are switched on by the uncertain stuff of human life and come alive when faced with life at its most uncontrollable.

Success-seeking Nowists naturally move towards opportunities for feeling effective in any circumstances. But in high-certainty situations they feel less exhilarated, and so the joy payoff is lower. And, as a result, Nowists tend to shift towards the thrills of success amid uncertainty because of the full-on pleasures that this brings.

Uncertainty suggests potential, and the prospect of proving self-potential against the odds, or against criticism, and it is this that can be alluring and inspiring. For example, consider the responses by self-diagnosed 'uncertainty-orientated' participants to two online advertisements after they were asked which they pre-ferred. One described a comedian with the tagline of 'being the next big thing' in the other the comedian was described as 'likely to become the next big thing'.[13] The second option came out on top. *Potential* was pre-ferred by Nowists.

Crucially it is this focus on potential that provides advantages not just in the now, but over the long term. The pursuit of uncertain success means that the worst the Nowist typically feels is a lack of joy when something does not go their way. This may seem simple, but for those with a Thenist mindset it can be the reverse – feelings of disappointment at the self rather than the result can plague the mind and cause future decisions to be affected.[14] The problem with a failure-fearing Thenist mindset is that it influences people to miss out on the delights of success. Under its influence, people also attempt to sidestep life's unavoidable uncertainty, an attempt that is futile, counterproductive and time-consuming.

Thenists are so busy saying no that *if* they are successful the best they can hope for is a kind of neutral non-joy, because joy is only available with a side-order of possible failure and the uncertainty that they avoid. They may benefit from the sensation of focus that comes from being actively engaged in work that is challenging, but the joy of now tends to be closed to them.

Nowists want change, and they want new, which is why they are more likely to be uncertainty-oriented. They want to try to succeed at new tasks that tell them something new about themselves, and keep alive that feeling of forward motion and self-enlightenment.

This comes from their need to have a clear run at challenges; naturally they either opt for situations where there are fewer constraints or simply act with fewer constraints in whatever situation they find themselves. So they pull down barriers to movement, make the pulling down of barriers part of their achievement, or find places where there are fewer obvious internal cultural barriers but where they are challenged to do work with uncertain outcomes.

Think of billionaire entrepreneur Elon Musk. As a twelve-year-old he sold computer software he had written for $500 to a magazine; as a 22-year-old he sold his stake in his first start-up for $22 million; and as a thirty-year-old he sold his share in PayPal for $165 million. Musk then immediately invested it all in a seemingly insane three-streamed plan to make solar power the dominant source of energy, convert the whole world to battery-driven cars, and colonise the moon. The point is less that Musk has succeeded in the past, and more that he was motivated each time to gamble his winnings on new ventures where final payback was uncertain.[15] For Musk it was not a gamble but an embrace of the uncertain.

The Nowist finds uncertainty motivating. Uncertainty is the often irresistible allure of a challenge that *may* fail. This possibility of failure can be because the challenge has never been attempted before, or because it is difficult enough to leave doubt about future success. Failure is an option. And it is this lack of certainty that energises Nowists to quickly start, continue and accomplish, before quickly starting again.

Nowists seek more than the absence of anxiety, and more than a sense of timeless hyper-focus: non-boredom is better than boredom, but not nearly as good as desire that moves to action.

FUN-LOVIN' TIME LORDS

Nowists use time to keep moving forward because they find pleasure in moving forward, so when you're in a Nowist mindset your relationship with time changes in a number of surprising ways.

Nowists feel that they are in control of their use of time, rather than time controlling them. They have powerful internal clocks so that they know how long different tasks will take; this means they can keep momentum because they don't find themselves missing out on connecting tasks. Like an experienced

YOUR LIFE IS WHAT HAPPENS WHEN YOU'RE BUSY TRYING TO BECOME UNBUSY

jetsetter or backpacker who knows the timetables and understands the nature of different forms of transport, the Nowist is naturally good at sequencing their own actions and the actions of others to get to the future on time.

Evidence for this came from a study by psychologists in Rome who looked at how people differed in their perceived control of time.[16] They found that too much Thenist-style focus on what might have been, and what might yet be, meant that those people no longer felt in control of their own actions in the present or of outcomes in the future.

And this makes a lot of sense. If you spend your time thinking about events in the past and future in a very general way you don't ever get back to considering the specific ways you can make things happen. And if you don't get the hang of doing things, moving from idea to action, then you will lack confidence in your ability to make things happen.

Instead of feeling at the mercy of uncontrollable time, the Nowist embraces time as a friend. They use past, present, and future to clear the way for actions that are as effortless as possible in the moment. They favour approaches that allow them to take action sooner, and strategies that provide streams of connected actions, so that they don't have to stop. They want to start now *and* keep moving.

For this reason, Nowists see the future as a stream of connected sequences of actions and decisions. Thinking this way – seeing choices as decisions that help them bridge between sequences of actions – means that they don't have to stop moving. Each decision is linked to many connected actions, so they don't have to make as many decisions. And they can enjoy the pleasure of seeing progress in the past, present and future, rather than discrete tasks that seem to add up to very little.

As Nowists learn to embrace their desire for movement, they learn not to run around aimlessly, but instead adjust the aim of their actions in a purposeful, more far-sighted, way. They plan, not because they love planning as such, but so that they can keep moving from activity to activity, enjoying the pay-off of individual tasks, and running purposively between them.[17]

They have a preference for doing many things at the same time[18] – and enjoy any chance to juggle different kinds of task[19] – because doing many things allows them to move faster, and because task-juggling allows them to stretch time to fit in more change.

THE WISDOM OF THRILL-SEEKERS

There's a lot of negative press about sensation-seeking, as if somehow wanting to experience intense sensations, like joy and excitement, is automatically a bad thing. Like impulsivity, it's often been assumed that all sensation-seeking, thrill-loving motivations are similar, and that they all lead somewhere negative.

With their natural desire to move forward, Nowists are particularly responsive to situations where the rewards come from the sensation of action or speed, rather than inaction or delay. It is unlikely that they would be content to sit in a very long, unproductive meeting, particularly when nothing is happening, and nothing is likely to happen. The lack of action is almost painful. As children, boredom made them fidget. As adults, Nowists become more skilled at creating their own opportunities for action, and making good things happen.

So when five hundred people working in a wide range of jobs, organisations and roles were assessed, researchers found two very different kinds of sensation-seekers: the anti-social and the entrepreneurial.[20] The anti-social escaped boredom, and got thrills, by causing trouble and upsetting other people. The entrepreneurially minded were able to get their kicks by testing themselves in the attempt to master new skills in the uncertain arena of competition. They found a cure for boredom.

In another insightful experiment a group of Nowists and Thenists were recruited.[21] They all watched a computer screen as a series of ninety-six two-digit numbers, from a set of twelve possible numbers, were shown in a random sequence on the screen.

Half of the numbers were designated as *bad* and half the numbers were designated as *good*. As a participant, you were asked to click on a button if you thought that the number was on the good list, but not to click if the number was on the bad list. You had to guess which were good and bad, and do so based on trial, error and partial on-screen feedback about whether your guesses were correct or incorrect.

One half of the participants – the reward group – were told about 80 per cent of the time if they had pressed the button correctly, and only 25 per cent of the time if they had been wrong to press the button. The other half – the punishment group – received feedback about wrong choices 80 per cent of the time and right choices 25 per cent of the time.

Nowists responded much more strongly to being told more often when they had guessed correctly. It was a natural fit because they want any information that helps them to keep moving – and positive feedback about the correct direction for their next leap or next guess is highly energising.

This instinct for looking while leaping keeps Nowists rolling onward and can become a significant advantage. Another clever experiment, by a team of neuroscientists in London and Oxford, explored the surprisingly powerful advantages that Nowists have in certain kinds of environment.[22] The researchers set up a traffic lights test in which a red light turned to amber and then green. The goal was to press a button as soon as the green light appeared. Participants received very small financial penalties if they pressed the button too soon, and bigger rewards the closer they could get to the light appearing. It was a test of their ability to anticipate, and to be willing to bet on their ability to anticipate. Who did best? People whose lack of premeditation meant that they didn't second-guess their way into second place.

GOT TO BE STARTING SOMETHING

Like sprinters who anticipate the start of a race, a key element behind a Nowist's ability to enjoy action is their ability to get started. And get started now.

In a Nowist mindset you are looking for whatever gets you moving: reasons to move; reasons to start; reasons to change; reasons to keep going; ways of keeping on, keeping on.

To make it easier to start, Nowists are better able to make the future feel like now.[23] And because it is easier to be motivated to start when the deadline is closer, they use Nowist mind tricks to make the task deadline seem like part of the present.[24]

In a real-world study, farmers were asked to meet deadlines for opening a savings account. One group was given the deadline of December, while the other group was given a deadline of January the next year. Although in reality the two deadlines were only a month apart, they were still able to change the behaviour of participants. December dates were treated as like the present, with farmers more likely to open the account immediately. Because January was regarded as unlike the present, farmers delayed starting.

As a Nowist, moving the priorities of your future-self into the present can become such a natural perspective that you are more likely to start something as early as possible than wait too long.

Wanting to start moving as soon as possible means that you're not really into that whole procrastination scene. In fact, you're much more likely to start immediately, even for a task when starting sooner might be less efficient or less convenient than starting later.

This desire to start immediately, despite the possibility of inefficiency, is a tendency that's been labelled precrastination. It was christened by a team of psychologists who made the unexpected discovery during a cleverly designed set of experiments involving two buckets of sand, an alley and a platform onto which one of the buckets could be placed.[25] Participants were asked to walk along, grab just one of the buckets and place it on the platform.

The researchers had expected people to pick up the bucket closest to the platform, because this would have been the least amount of effort. Instead, participants were much more likely to pick up the bucket closest to them, even if that meant carrying the bucket over a longer distance. There was a definite preference for just getting started and saving thinking time and mental energy for the next task.

With more experience, Nowists start to create more time – and space – for smooth, effortless forward motion: keeping what they need within easy reach, doing immediately what will have to be done eventually. Moving fast, then slow, but always looking at effortless paths for leaping forward.

You can see this pattern in the approach of the world's very best rock climbers. They feel almost nervous, emotionally and mentally switched on before the climb. They look ahead while others are looking down. They are seeing the route ahead, not just as individual holds, or the top and bottom, but instead as combinations of holds and problems. They are looking ahead for the crux of the particular climb – so that they can be preparing while ascending.

A team of psychologists found that the winners of international speed-climbing competitions climb faster on the simple parts of the climb, and start moving more slowly just before reaching the crux.[26] They look ahead to save strength for the leap. And that's smart because there is often a leap required, a part of the challenge that cannot be overcome unless you move fast and fluidly.

Novices climb at the same speed at all points of the climb until they get stuck. They try to edge upward but exhaust themselves. They can't see the nature of the problem from so close, and missed out on the opportunity to look from a distance when they were still on the ground. An unsighted climber can become stuck and tired as fatigue builds unpleasantly in muscles, from quivering fingertips to trembling calves. They hang there, afraid to fall, afraid to jump, any effort too timid or too erratic to be anything other than self-defeating.

THE MAGIC OF MORNINGS

David Bowie would use the magic of early mornings to create space for looking while leaping. He'd wake at 4 a.m., and walk quietly downstairs, make himself a coffee while everyone else was sleeping. Read the paper, clear his mind, let his mind wander, effortlessly preparing alternative paths forward. He loved those early still mornings because of their power for priming perpetual movement.

Early mornings are friends to Nowists who want to slide in friction-free, high-energy mode into each day. And that's what studies have found – that high locomotors are also much more likely to be morningness-oriented.[27] They tend to value getting started before the pressures of the day build, and can enjoy time free of demands. Even knowing about the power of those extra hours can free up the Nowist to move enjoyably through the experience-rich actions of the day.

It is one reason that Nowists are as likely to work effortlessly into the night, because they love to keep their locomoting groove going. And because they love many things and love moving *between* streams of what they love, they tend towards harmonious passion rather than stressful obsession.[28]

In one study, Italian students were asked to complete a set of questions about their morningness preferences and their locomotion tendencies – it found a strong correlation between the two. The authors speculated on how the two preferences might be mutually reinforcing, since morningness might come from a desire to get moving and a desire to get moving might get someone moving early in the morning. They also speculated, as we've done, about how locomotors are likely to flexibly seek motion through morningness and eveningness.

And so one of our Nowists embraces a full day working alongside his employees, then rolls into landscaping his garden until he's laying paving stones and edging the lawn in the dark, pushing to get it ready before his own fiftieth-birthday garden party, sharing a beer and some laughter with his family on the deck, before cheerfully waking at 4 a.m. to complete some of the paperwork needed by his clients. He's not stressed, he's loving it.

Nowists recognise the dangers of obsessive passion. Their belief in forward motion and action over inaction allows them to be flexible when in the crux of a situation. This flexibility allows for the path to grow as they go – it pushes them towards other goals, or opportunities, that they feel are equally important – even if those other actions mean switching their attention. It may take a moment, or maybe longer, but they are better able to see the value in more than only one narrowly monotonous obsession.

Nowists get passionate about what they do, but because they love what they do, and enjoy action for its intrinsic pleasure, they are much more likely to experience passion without the negative stress.

So they find it easier to train and complete a marathon than others, because the desire to run comes as much from joy in movement as any desire to be fit or impress others. And that's a great complement to the effort involved in running for miles and miles, day after day.

They may also work more hours than other people, past the point that some people would see as healthy, but their locomoting delight in the work itself often re-energises in a way that protects, or buffers, them from becoming burnt out. The movement, the task, the physical or mental exertion can leave them happily tired rather than emotionally and existentially drained.[29]

NOWIST STRESS CLOCK

Nowists are able to keep moving forward because they become skilled at regulating their own stress levels. They get better at recognising the signs of burnout, and dialling down their response to stress, their commitments or their workload.

Pushing your limits is what allows you to grow stronger, so if you find yourself feeling passive, it can make sense to dial it up a little. Get moving. Accomplish something small. Do something you enjoy. Embrace what moves you. And start again.

You can push to the limits for short bursts, but if you push too far there will be negative consequences. You can suffer high levels of distress, or even hyper-stress, that make you feel weak and brittle, at just those times when you need to be most powerful and flexible.

If you find yourself overwhelmed, or realise you have an impossible level of commitments, you have a choice, and the stress clock helps you remember that choice. Pin up a copy or draw your own version. You can find a healthy place, full of energy, full of belief in your ability to make good things happen.

You can learn to let go of tasks and expectations that will weaken rather than strengthen you. You can get help from others to spread the load. You are able to look ahead and get stronger ahead of the future challenges.

We can all sometimes take on too much. We may feel stuck with our commitments but unable to complete them. In a Nowist mindset we learn how to let go of what slows us down, including our own desires to work too hard, expect perfection, or please everyone.

THE REGRET MINIMISATION STRATEGY

Naturally, given Nowists' speed-loving, uncertainty-craving attitudes and behaviour, life in Nowist mode is likely to include mistakes, failures, crises, accidents and mishaps. Not everything is going to work, and they don't want a life where everything is successfully boring.

Jeff Bezos famously stated that he started Amazon. com as part of his regret minimisation strategy. He said that he thought about being eighty years old, and looking back on his life. He concluded that he would never regret having created an Internet start-up even if it failed, but that he would regret having not tried to make his idea work.

The action-oriented Nowist is also the regret-minimising Nowist. It is why they seek to avoid the regret of inaction, looking back and wondering what might have happened if they had acted. It is also why they find it easier to sidestep letting the one that got away stopping them from enjoying the next opportunity.

This second kind of response can really slow people down because there are so many opportunities that appear to have been missed. And for people in a Thenist mindset, the pain of missing out once tends to drag focus away from all the opportunities that are available, so you lose out more than once.

You'll probably remember the feeling. You don't get selected for a team, or get hired for a job, and so you don't try out for another team, or apply for the thousands of other jobs. Regretting the one that got away wastes energy that would be better invested on the many opportunities still to be discovered and enjoyed.

When psychologists looked at this response to missing out on an opportunity, several different experiments confirmed that people generally devalue new opportunities because they compare them to the missed opportunity. It happened whether people missed out on special offer at a health gym, or a bargain price for a luxury guided tour of a foreign city.[30] They couldn't see past what had been lost.

Action is rarely effortless for a person in a Thenist mindset because they spend so much of their energy worrying. They worry about that missed opportunity, and what they might have said, or done, to the point that they miss out on subsequent opportunities. They also worry about wasting time or effort, or money that they have already spent. So much so that a Thenist may waste moments they can never get back worrying about wasted opportunities that they can never get back.

This kind of worry and self-criticism can really mess with your life. When heavyweight boxer Shannon Briggs lost a title fight, he became so fixated on what he had not gained that he stopped moving forward, started eating junk food, and gained one hundred and fifty pounds of unhealthy fat. He missed out on million-dollar paycheques, playing with his kids, and just having fun. After seeing himself in a mirror, he said to himself, 'Let's go, Champ!' That moment of #Now was enough for him to get moving. By moving forward, he lost the weight, challenging himself with the same phrase, 'Let's go, Champ,' shouting it out until it became a battle cry, and until he became a contender again.

Nowists grab the opportunities that are available now, rather than worrying about what is past. Which is why they are more able to step past loss to embrace whatever is happening now and next. It's also why they can change direction, even when that means letting go of what they have already invested.

If you've already spent time and energy on something, it is tempting to keep spending, even after it makes no sense. You can't get the time, energy or money back, but it can be so hard to let go. This is known as the sunk cost fallacy, and it's something that people are pretty much immune to when they are in a Nowist mindset. In a classic test of sunk cost fallacy, you are asked to imagine you are an executive for an aircraft corporation and given a dilemma to solve.

In the first version of the dilemma you have already invested one hundred million dollars into a spy plane that can evade radar when you learn that your competitor has just launched their own version that is clearly better than yours. Will you spend another ten million dollars to complete the plane?

In the second version of the dilemma, an employee suggests that you should spend ten million dollars on developing a spy plane that can evade radar, even though your competitor has just launched a better version of the same idea. Again, will you spend ten million dollars to develop the plane?

Results showed that people are generally biased towards investing more money if they have already committed themselves financially. Many people are so eager to protect their investment that they can't think clearly. They are trapped in the chase to protect what they have already spent. Nowists responded differently. They showed no bias towards protecting the investment. Instead, they were able to choose to invest or not based on whatever they felt was the smartest way forward.

This is because Nowists don't waste time looking backwards, because that's not where they're going. They are good at bringing what they want from the past – including lessons from their previous experiences and good memories – rather than having to live in the past. They pack light to go fast. And once they're moving effortlessly forward, they keep looking ahead so that they can keep moving forward.

JOY OF
#NOW

OVERWHELMED

too much
stress energy

not enough
stress energy

UNDERPOWERED

CHAPTER 3
BECAUSE EFFORTLESS
IS NOT LAZY

Nowists prefer effortless decisions. There is nothing lazy in their preference for effortless decisions, nor are they demonstrating childish or immature reasoning. Their effortless decisions rely on what some view as more advanced cognitive systems – neural networks that develop throughout and beyond childhood. Children generally rely on computational reasoning (going through the detail), whereas adults switch to employing intuitional reasoning (knowing what the detail means). It's not that we can't compute more painstakingly, it's just that we don't, and for a very good reason.

THE PERFECT PIZZA PARTY PROBLEM

There are a few principles that guide a preference for effortless thinking. The first is understanding that the pains taken are not always worth the effort: near enough can be good enough. If you know that you need about two slices of pizza per person, and that each pizza can provide eight slices, about five pizzas is a decent approximation for a party of twenty people. Going with five pizzas because you had five pizzas last time for pretty much the same crew is even faster. Imagine the pain of calculating anything much more accurately – you could have a supercomputer with the best mathematical modellers in the world and still struggle to find the perfect quantity of pizzas to order. How many people are likely to drop out? What will they have eaten before they arrive? Who will be dieting? Even if you could somehow calculate the perfect number of pizzas to order, that figure could change at any moment – it is vulnerable to fluctuating with every bite one of your guests takes.

Faced with this level of complexity, some people still try to solve the perfect pizza problem and get stuck in an infinite loop of possibilities, none of which are calculable. An unenjoyable waste of time that could been better spent doing something like actually ordering the pizza, or putting up the lights on the deck, or being inspired to buy fireworks as you move from task to fulfilling task.

The second principle that underlies this kind of approach is the knowledge that computations may know the sums of everything and the meaning of nothing. The neural networks that develop throughout childhood use two kinds of memory – a shallow, facts-only, verbatim memory and a deep, meanings-mainly, gist memory. When we reach adolescence, we are most likely to use our facts-only memory, and reason in the way that an economist might assume. We may take what seems like a crazy risk to an adult, because we have calculated the risk without understanding the meaning of that risk.

So an adolescent brain might figure that unprotected sex is unlikely to result in either pregnancy or disease, and proceed. Or calculate the probability of a car crash, and not bother with a seat belt. Or compute the likelihood of lung cancer, and light up a cigarette as a result.[31] If you keep to computational probabilities only, even the craziest of risks – like Russian roulette – may not seem so crazy if you don't factor in the rather final meaning of death.

There is convincing evidence for this approach to reasoning and memory, some of which comes from the surprising conclusions drawn from fascinating experiments devised by neuroscientist Valerie Reyna and

NOWISTS
BELIEVE
THAT
DONE
IS BETTER THAN
PERFECT

her colleagues.[32] In one such experiment,[33] participants, many of them statistics students, were presented
with a problem involving two boxes, which they were
told contained a mixture of red and blue marbles. Box
X always contained 10 marbles – 9 red and 1 blue. The
proportions of marbles in box Y varied.

> In box Y, there were either:
> (a) 95 marbles, 85 red and 10 blue, or
> (b) 100 marbles, 90 red and 10 blue, or
> (c) 105 marbles, 95 red and 10 blue.

For each of the alternative values of box Y, participants
had to either decide whether box X or box Y gave
them the best chance of picking a red marble, or simply state that it didn't matter which box was chosen.
Half of the participants were given no time limit to
complete the task, and took different amounts of time
depending on the proportions of marbles contained
in box Y. Option (a) took longest, about 37 seconds,
then option (c), 31 seconds, with option (b) the
quickest at 17 seconds. The other half of the group
only had 10 seconds to read and answer the problem.
Surprisingly, as researchers noted, participants
responded correctly 65 per cent of the time when self-
paced and 64 per cent when under time pressure.
How could this be?

It turned out that the people who performed best relied on effortless, gist-based, fast thinking. High performers used more time when more time was available, but whatever they did with it, they didn't need the extra time to answer correctly.

Their decisions were fast *and* accurate, which leads to the surprising conclusion that people – our Nowists – who are willing to put speed ahead of accuracy may rarely be making an accuracy sacrifice, because accuracy doesn't depend on being slow. The truth is that time spent going slow – thinking too much and trying to find the perfect answer – is often worse than wasted.

If our second-guessing, momentum-robbing, Thenist mindsets take over, they get parts of our brains involved that are unhelpful for making effortless decisions.

SCATTERGUN SLOW

Consider what happened when a team of neuroscientists recruited people to take what's called an n-back test. Participants were shown a succession of 3D shapes on screen, and then asked, at various points, whether the shape currently before them matched, or didn't match, a shape shown a number of steps back.[34]

The results showed that people who are particularly fast and accurate used a very precise set of working memory regions in the prefrontal cortex of the brain. The slower people, who made more errors, had a more scattergun approach, getting unhelpful areas of the brain involved – parts that are needed for conflict control, or parts like the default mode network, discussed later in this book, that are linked to generating hypotheticals or musing about identity. These were less relevant, even distracting, and interfered with their performance. Put more simply, the task at hand didn't get good Nowist attention because Thenist brain functions were brought into play at the wrong time.

This finding is similar to the simpler ideas put forward by Tim Gallwey in his classic book *The Inner Game of Tennis*. There are two selves, he argued, and when one gets in the way, performance suffers. Performance, he said, is ability minus interference. Whatever you are worrying or daydreaming about subtracts from whatever you are trying to do.

He didn't have the benefit of evidence from brain scans or insights from cognitive psychology, but he did have first-hand experience of observing tennis players. He was interested in those top athletes who shared the same level of skill and physical prowess, but still performed very differently. They should have won and lost more or less equally, with only random chance separating their records, but instead one would win, or lose, much more often than the other. To one, the championship, to the other the runners-up prize, or barely staying high enough in the rankings to remain on the professional tour.

Think of Murray cursing into his hand, or yelling in anguish up at his team, while Djokovic or Federer effortlessly defeat him. The difference isn't physical. For tennis, Murray is almost the perfect athlete, the equal or near equal of Djokovic, who is only a week younger; but Murray is only victorious when his actions are automatic and smooth.

There's a reason why Djokovic has beaten him in four grand slam finals, and why Federer has won all three grand slam finals in which they have faced one another. That reason appears to explain why Murray hired Amélie Mauresmo as coach: when he sat down with her he 'found her very calming'. It also, perhaps, explains why he stopped working with her after less than a year.[35] And why his list of self-leading, self-motivating quotes includes the reminder to 'Be Good to Yourself'. [36]

Thinking beyond the point, beyond the rally, beyond the match, gets in the way of Murray's ability. By getting ahead of himself, he sabotages his own Nowness. In his own words he described the moment when he realised that Djokovic was struggling physically in the 2015 Australian Open men's final: 'I was thinking – "Oh, my God, this could be yours. If someone is cramping in the final of a Grand Slam, the match is yours."' But

Murray lost. For the third time. Instead of clarity, reward in the moment or rapid calm, he, like many of us, has to struggle with panic, overwhelming sensations that lead to recklessness. And, so often, this kind of Thenist over-thinking leads to unthinking outbursts that overcome that feeling of rightness in the moment.

This same feeling of rightness can allow someone to smoothly make the right sequence of decisions and actions in any given situation: whether you're relaxed on holiday or playing with your children; time-pressured at work, or task-pressured flying a jet; or both time-pressured *and* task-pressured when saving a life in an emergency.

Again, the evidence is strong for individual differences in the effortlessness of people's thinking when faced with challenging or urgent tasks. A test of this, similar to the n-back test, is to ask people to look at a photograph and then tell you when subsequent photographs either match or don't match. When researchers did exactly this, they found that low performers find it harder to dial down the Thenist network in the brain,[37] the part that interferes with your ability to be in the present and that voices the *what-ifs* and *might-have-beens*, processing hypothetical thoughts about yourself and others. This is good stuff. It does valuable work. But it does its best work between tasks, and around tasks. It provides your Nowist network with options for action, but it gets in the way when it starts whispering, or even yelling, alternatives like a demented back-seat-driver from hell.

HELL IS BACK-SEAT DRIVERS

Sartre says that 'hell is other people', or, more accurately, 'hell is the others.'[38] By this he is referring to the pain of being judged by the distorted, negative views of others. This includes what we think the 'others' think, but also the negative, distorted views of ourselves by our own others – our past, future and present selves. In our example, the back-seat driver is a whole series of self-related, time-related thoughts that can make now hellish.

This kind of back-seat driving can overwhelm our better judgement so that we are busy arguing with our various selves rather than calmly moving forward. In a recent study this was also shown to be the case with novice drivers, who made decisions too slowly to keep up with the road conditions and then lurched into action, leading to more accidents and deaths. Instead it was the experienced drivers who made faster decisions – calmly and quickly anticipating and reacting; keeping in time with the flow of the surrounding traffic. Just as experienced Nowists keep up with the speed and flow of life.

BECAUSE EFFORTLESS IS NOT LAZY

The novice drivers acted more like Jordan Spieth, who lost in the final round of the 2016 US Masters.[39] He dropped six shots in only three holes because 'indecision over where to drop the ball played havoc with his mindset'. He should have calmly, and quickly, moved into the next shot. Instead he was distracted and slowed down by regrets over the last shot.[40] Jordan said he rushed, yet it would be more accurate to say he choked – and that's quite a different thing. It's not speed that Nowists avoid, but the painful crash.

The distinction between speed and smooth, and between rapid and reckless, is also useful when you're a professional NFL football player. You can't just slow down and take a moment to make the right decision when a 300-pound super athlete is going to cover the 40 yards between you in the next five seconds or so.[41] Panic is bad, effortless decisions are good.

It's become standard practice in the NFL to pick players who have scored high on a twelve-minute, fifty-question test (known as the Wonderlic after its original author) that claims to measure aptitude for learning and problem solving. Some commentators have asserted that success on the test will predict performance in the professional game.[42]

The problem is, it doesn't. More detailed research has found that the reverse is often true.[43] In most of the important career statistics, if you scored higher on

the Wonderlic, you were less likely to perform well in your rookie year *and* less likely to keep improving over your career.

So what does make a difference? Helpfully, another researcher assessed NFL football players for dysfunctional impulsivity and Dickman's functional impulsivity at the start of a season.[44] At the end of the season, statistics were collected, including data about injuries, game penalties, points scored and games played. What they found surprised them, but will no longer surprise anyone reading this book. Players with the highest levels of dysfunctional impulsivity tended to perform worse, suffer the most head injuries, be penalised more often by officials during the game, and show more aggression outside of the game. For players with higher levels of functional impulsivity, the reverse pattern was found. They had fewer injuries, especially serious injuries, and were capable of 'split-second decisions' that could 'take advantage of unexpected opportunities'. As a result, they were more likely to be viewed positively by their coaches, and to play better and start games.

TRUSTING YOUR INNER NOWIST

Nowists tend to make split-second decisions with good outcomes, in part because of their willingness to trust their overall sense of what needs to be done in a

situation. They delegate authority to their precon-
scious, which is able to focus attention on the level of
detail needed to make a decision – and find an action
that fits the situation.

To do this they clear their minds of the irrelevant
– anything that gets in the way of clearly seeing what
needs to be done next, and then get on with it.
Negative emotions related to mistakes, whether they
occurred long ago or in the past few seconds – and
even if they played a part in causing the situation you
now face – are better left behind, or downplayed.

So if you get action-oriented Nowists to try almost
anything, they will handle mistakes better than other
people, especially when everyone involved really
wants to succeed. In laboratory conditions, psychologists in Holland explored how well four different
groups managed their emotions, and performance,
after making errors. The tests[45] involved looking at a
row of letters and deciding whether the middle letter
in the row was the same as, or different from, the rest
of the letters.[46]

Half the group were Nowists by nature, half were
Thenists who tended to worry about the difference
between what is and what can be or could have been.
In addition, the researchers ingeniously designed the
experiment to encourage half of each group to be more
interested in winning, because they would be paid for

success, and half more focused on avoiding losing, because they would be penalised financially for making errors.[47]

People with a more action-oriented Nowist approach were better able to shrug off the negative emotions from getting something wrong, and had an even *bigger* advantage when they were rewarded for success. They could see past any negative back-seat driving and keep moving forward, because they naturally recognised the benefits were tipped in favour of future, and present, opportunities to succeed.

This was the perfect fit between what Nowists want, which is a sense of moving forward, and what is on offer – an immediate pay-off.

But there is something else that Nowists believe about making mistakes. Not only do they instinctively move past distracting, or passive, negativity, they also take with them useful lessons from the experience of making a mistake.[48] And, unlike many people, Nowists know that taking action is often the best way of helping you to decide both what you *can* do next and what you *want* to do next.[49] This is counterintuitive to some people, who want to decide what they want to try without trying anything.

Nowists take advantage of action as a kind of mental shortcut.[50] First, by making a choice – to do something – they learn what actions lead to what outcomes, and gain practical skills in the art of making something happen: it's an education in cause and effect. And they develop the habit of moving from choice to decision, and come to understand how it feels – both the good and the bad.

Second, Nowists learn more about their own preferences in terms both of the action *and* the outcome. You can link the action with a consequence and the outcome to a preference. You go to a party, and have a good time, so you remember that going to a party is something you enjoy. Or you taste squid and have an allergic reaction, so you remember that squid is something that could kill you. The result is a valuable store of patterns for later decisions. Each action-outcome pattern can be used with confidence because you have already used it – and because you know how you *feel* about it. With the added bonus that having new experiences is more enjoyable to Nowists than thinking about whether to have new experiences.

In a sense, everyone has access to this kind of learning, but not everyone embraces it equally. In the world of chess, it's been clearly shown that grandmasters, the best of the best, have as many as one hundred thousand different move combinations stored in their heads, ready for use. They acquire those patterns for future action by taking action. From playing and playing – from *doing*. And when they are thinking of which move to make next, they are able to rapidly recognise the situation, and match it to a pattern that fits.[51]

There are other ways of acquiring action-outcome patterns. You can read about them, you can watch other people, you can imagine them, you can role-play – the closer your learning comes to real-world action, the closer it is to giving you the fluency of action-experience.

Many top athletes imagine many of the details very specifically before they go into action. They try to get as close as they can to real life, so that they recognise what to do when their moment of #Now arrives. Listen to Wayne Rooney speaking about how he uses imag-ination to make action effortless:

> Part of my preparation is I go and ask the kit man what colour we're wearing – if it's red top, white shorts, white socks or black socks. Then I lie in bed the night before the game and visualise myself scoring goals or doing well. You're trying to put yourself in that moment and trying to prepare yourself, to have a 'memory' before the game. I don't know if you'd call it visualising or dreaming, but I've always done it, my whole life.[52]

He would imagine not only before the game, but during the game. He explains that even on the pitch, 'You've got to think three or four passes where the ball is going to come to down the line. And the very best footballers, they're able to see that before – much quicker than a lot of other footballers.'

Nowists believe in all those forms of learning – but they are drawn to direct experience because it can reach parts that no other learning can. So, in the hours leading up to game-time, Stephen Curry, voted the most valuable player in the National Basketball Association (and viewed by many as the 'greatest shooter of all time'[53]), goes to the court, where he takes more than a hundred shots. Why? Because he wants to 'just see the ball going into the net'. And then he starts taking shots from over fifty feet away, off the court, nearer the locker rooms than the hoop.

This time it is about the enjoyment of uncertainty, trying to do what is fun, testing himself.

It is learning that is living – not learning while waiting to live.

Take, as another example, fast chess, which has been criticised by some serious players of the game for not being sufficiently serious.[54] It was, however, a great passion of chess genius Mikhail Tal, who holds the world record for the first- and second-longest unbeaten runs in competitive chess history, and is known for being 'the best attacking player of all time'. Tal loved to play the game. He didn't look down on the ultra-fast version, but valued it both for the sheer pleasure of playing and for the way in which it accelerated his learning of new patterns that helped him play better.[55]

In a game of fast chess, players can have as little as five minutes each to finish all their moves, compared to between ninety minutes and six hours for traditional tournament games.[56] Bullet chess can be even faster – with only thirty seconds per player.

What Mikhail's love of fast chess reveals is a somewhat Nowist approach to living his life and playing the game. He explained that he preferred to 'play chess than to study it' and always prioritised 'seizing the initiative from his opponents'. He was willing to embrace 'unavoidable errors', because 'if you wait for luck to turn up, life becomes very boring.' And so he became famous for sacrificing material for initiative,[57] which means being willing to lose individual pieces if it allowed him to gain overall momentum in the game, with whole sequences of his games described as 'wild tactical melees with speculative sacrifices'.[58]

In some delightful research by psychologists in Florida into the differences between stronger and weaker chess players, it was found that when given

THE BEST
THINGS
HAPPEN
TO THOSE WHO
DON'T
WAIT

easy, medium and difficult chess problems, the stronger players *and* the weaker players all did better with more time.[59] Presented with a number of chess pieces set up in a particular way in front of them, they were asked to come up with their best move. Given five minutes to describe both the first move that came to mind, and their thought process for choosing their best move, most players said that the first move that came to mind was the first pattern they recognised that fitted the situation. On average, the strong players were better at all levels of difficulty, which is an unsurprising combination of talent and years of practice. We already knew they were better. What is more interesting is that the *first* move of the expert players was almost always better than the *best* move of the weakest players. The expert players had an advantage at *any* speed.

Another way that Nowists are able to make fluent sequences of generally painless decisions is that they are comfortable with the principle of 'better done than perfect'. They assess themselves against reasonable standards, set against their ability and situation in any particular time period – particularly the near future, where they can directly influence what happens.

It becomes easier and more enjoyable to make fluid decisions when you're not afraid of failure. And with a realistic appraisal of the situation it becomes easier not to be distracted by unlikely failure. This goes back to what we were discussing earlier, and will discuss later in chapter 5 – Nowists set up a sustainable spiral of success by neatly side-stepping unhelpful emotional distress.

loss
regret
worry

#

past

growth

joy

pportunity

reward

obstacle

future

PART TWO
THE THREE STREAMS OF #NOW

CHAPTER 4
THERE'S ONLY ONE WAY TO FIND OUT

Just as every atom contains massive energy, so each moment of #Now contains power.

First, your personal power, your energy and self-belief to keep moving. Your ability to slip smoothly past the obstacles and things slowing you down by using the flux of life to propel you perpetually forward.

Second, your power to influence others to get more done. Your ability to attract help and supporters, to attract friends, partners, backers, a fan club; to get more done than you could ever do alone.

And third, the fundamental power of moving, the power of (automatic) momentum to make things happen. The cumulative, multiplicative, holistic power of #Now, as you keep rolling forward, in powerful spirals of joyful action and growth.

AN INITIAL STEP IS TO REALISE AND RECOGNISE THE POWERFUL DIFFERENCE BETWEEN GOALS AND ANTI-GOALS

Goals are the things you want. Things that are desirable and worth seeking out – they may be based on a wish or a dream, but they are best when they are actively motivational. You'll compare where you are with what you want, find a gap and respond emotionally and then, perhaps, directionally – you may act differently to move towards your goal.

Anti-goals are the things you do not want. They are undesirable, to be avoided – ought-nots, fears, nightmares, unattractive or, worse, de-motivational in a way that drains you of energy. You'll compare where you are with what you don't want, see a gap, and respond emotionally, and then directionally – you may act differently to move away from your unwanted anti-goal.

There are countless goals and anti-goals, and they compete for attention and energy. We all differ in what turns us on, or drives us away. We also differ in whether goals or anti-goals are most likely to influence our behaviour. And our goals and anti-goals can be connected so that achieving a goal requires the experience of an anti-goal. Or avoiding an anti-goal means sacrificing the longed-for satisfaction of the goal.

You may hate being told what to do – an anti-goal – but love being able to accomplish more as part of a team. You may love doing great work that requires resources – a goal – but hate asking for money – an anti-goal. Or you may hate deadlines, but love accomplishment.

One kind of anti-goal avoidance is said to involve self-control. The standard approach to not doing something is to view self-control as actively using a limited energy resource to, again, actively resist. The anti-goal is often portrayed as something pleasurable, or easy, a distractor, compared to the many desired, better-for-you goals available.[60]

This perspective has in large part been informed by a famous experiment where people used up limited self-control energy to eat what they presumably viewed as distinctly non-yummy raw radishes. After using up their energy, they found it harder to successfully resist chocolate – the anti-goal on offer.

But is actively resisting an anti-goal really such a great use of precious energy? Just focusing on resisting the chocolate is a waste of energy. All the time you're looking hungrily over at the chocolate, or any other desirable anti-goal, the best you can hope for is a neutral result. You have *not* eaten, partaken, given in, but you are now behind because energy has been used for no specific goal benefit. Not eating chocolate does not equal fitness or health. Not doing something cannot bring the joy of doing something.

To keep resisting is exhausting, and the best-case scenario is un-living. It is much more rewarding to actively seek out the goal – the action – that will make it easy to avoid the anti-goal. So, for instance, exercise makes it easier to resist high-fat food. First, if you go for a run then it's unlikely that there will be a refrigerator-microwave combo in sight, or in mind. And second, the running often diminishes your interest in the anti-goal. You're less interested in the dopamine released by eating when you're getting high on the endorphins produced by exercise instead.

ENERGY IS LIFE. MOVEMENT IS LIVING

Calm energy is what we feel when we are bursting with a sense of power, deliciously blended with both the absence of worry and the presence of oneness with what we are doing – of nowness with our goals and actions. It's that blissed-out yet active state experienced by dancers or skateboarders, or any of us, when we are loving the exact thing we are doing in the #Now.

No-one is looking at the clock, because there is both never enough time and always enough time. A timeless state in which more is experienced, and more can be accomplished. If you do check your watch, you're amazed at how much has happened in such a short time. But you have no need to do so because you're in the joy of #Now.

People need energy to get things done. Some people find that tense energy, with its stressed movement, is a good thing because they enjoy that feeling of purpose and purposefulness. And it's why they may wait for deadlines to force them into action – external or internal pressures that keep them moving when there never seems to be enough time.

The trouble is that they may overdo it, they may overload, and even burn out. Their actions are driven by an obsessive, rather than harmonious passion.

It's one of the reasons that people may suddenly feel a harsh, even brutal, comedown after tension-filled highs. They feel tension-filled tiredness when they don't have the resources necessary to respond to that pressure of being forced forward. You'll feel depressed or pessimistic regardless of whether you've made progress or not.

We all tend to hit what distance runners call 'the wall'; some of us earlier and more often than others, some of us later and much more devastatingly. This is particularly true for those of us who are unable to turn smoothly back from over-exertion. This leads to the mental, emotional and physical damage that comes from becoming over-focused or over-stretched.[61] It is entirely different from the calm tired feeling that comes after calm energetic effort towards a reasonable goal.[62] On these occasions you enjoy the doing and are good to yourself, reminding yourself of how far you've come, or how being unhappy helps no-one, or of any of the many small beauties of the everyday.

This joy-leaning self-leadership is not automatic for all of us, but it can become more habitual. We can learn the ability to remind ourselves that well-being is not a second-class goal, and that meaning is to be found in enjoying the natural pleasures of life.

By keeping your energy flowing into movement, you are able to keep looking while leaping. You can live without the kind of self-defeating tension that can leave you with a headache, stiff muscles or that mystery pain in your back. Instead of chronic levels of cortisol, the hormone that kicks in when you feel stressed, you get an enjoyable spiral of adrenaline, dopamine and action.

GETTING STRONGER, EXTENDING YOUR #NOW

Nowists know that to feel strong at any particular moment is easier if you get stronger before each successive moment.

This getting stronger can be about your personal power, your ability to get things done. It can be about investing some of your energy into gaining extra know-how.

This can be the kind of know-how-to-do-something that comes from reading books, watching how-to videos online, or copying the way other people have done something.

It can be the kind of know-how-to-motivate-yourself that we've been talking about. The self-talk that leads to an action-oriented bias to movement.

But it can also be the kind of know-how-to-get-help-and-supporters that expands your strength to include other people's energy and knowledge. The kind of influence that extends your personal power by connecting it to the power of others. You feel stronger because you are not alone, and you are stronger because others are working alongside you.

In a Thenist mindset, those who feel alone are more likely to continue to be alone because they are unable to generate the energy to seek or attract help. They feel too weak to become stronger, so that rather than investing what strength they have to recruit others, they worry themselves into isolated passivity.

Even behind what seem the most individual pursuits, those who enjoy the most success, and enjoy their

success the most, are often those who attract and benefit from a network of fans and supporters.

Consider high diving. One individual, balanced on toes or fingertips, pushing upwards, once, twice, before springing into the shape of the first movement. Accelerating at 32 feet per second, performing somersaults and twists, then reaching 35 miles an hour in the 30 feet before decelerating to almost zero as they hit the water.

If the diver gets it right they will smoothly enter the water, hands palm-down, creating a space through which the rest of their body can enter. Hardly a splash, with a soft noise, the so-called 'rip entry', the muffled sound of tissue paper being torn – the cue for celebration or even victory.

Yet, as alone as the diver looks, there is a team of supporters who influence the success of the diver in that fleeting three seconds of gymnastic power.

Think of the British diver Tom Daley, who with each twist and somersault of his life gained support that expanded and multiplied his personal power. He was first inspired by a Canadian diver, who had won a gold medal at a young age and became Tom's hero – expanding his sense of what was possible. With the support of his parents he joined a diving course where he was fast-tracked into an elite team led by a coach with powerful ambitions of his own. With his parents and coaches behind him, he won his first senior medals aged eleven, acquiring support with every spin and twist.

This powerful support helped him win a medal at the 2012 Olympics. It also helped when he developed an aversion to performing one of his highest-scoring dive combinations, a problem caused by a camera flash going off during one of his dives at the Olympics. As a result, the dive he was attempting became a 'demon dive'. It was something that could have trapped him, but he used the support of fans to keep his belief high, and the advice of his team to get him therapy from a sports psychologist, and then a new coach. And together they moved forward again, leaving behind the old dive, all those hours and all that effort, to develop a new dive that helped win a gold medal at the world championships.[63]

It's easier to smoothly roll forward with the space and power that can come from supporters – those who give you the psychological room to see clearly; experts – those with knowledge that you lack; and veterans – those who have already experienced what you are going through, or can help you anticipate what may happen next. In this way, you can adjust your movement without either crashing or losing momentum.

So when Mark 'Facebook' Zuckerberg went to California, he recognised the value in the experience of Shawn Fanning, who had transformed the music industry by helping people share music online. His music-sharing company, Napster, was shut down by a legal challenge that actually made Fanning's experience even more useful to Zuckerberg.

Artists from Andy Warhol to Michelangelo have had rich support networks – teams of people behind the scenes to assist, inspire, coach, do the heavy lifting or the heavy selling. David Hockney, considered by many to be the greatest living British artist, has a team around him and lives in a converted boarding house with rooms to accommodate his many helpers. He has a warehouse close-by where frames and canvases can be made and larger works completed.

Even rivalries, like that between Henri Matisse and Pablo Picasso, can be part of what energises movement – they swapped artwork, studio visits and not always friendly challenges to outdo each other in a mutually beneficial provocation that lasted more than fifty years.

This space, this spiral, of nowness can be expanded or compressed, linear or exponential, shrunk or grown. And while the individual is always at the centre of their own #Now, they can extend its power by extending their own power through and with others. It is collaboration at its highest point of success.

The exact combination of self-talk, anxiety, looking

and leaping will vary. People who are motivated by the doing are more often able to enjoy better outcomes.

The most successful athletes tend to become proactively energised earlier than those who are less successful. At the year mark, the one-month mark and the one-day mark, their early-warning reminder system kicks in. Their background ability to look ahead comes to the foreground and alerts them to the need to prepare. They recognise the purpose of the feeling and move smoothly to work. Calm energy that propels them forward.

Less successful athletes tend to have less effective reminder systems or are less effective at using them. They think they have more time than they have, and fail to get working. They may overwork because they are fearful. Or hide from their fears and ignore the warning. Then, with an hour or a few seconds to go, they find it harder to manage their anxieties, which are now usually completely useless. Their alarms sound too late, too long and too generally; taking their mind away from the moment, to what they should or shouldn't have done, to their friends, their critics and coaches. Panic instead of calm.

GET MOVING, START ENJOYING

If you are stuck or overwhelmed the smart thing is to get unstuck and start rolling forward. And by far the easiest, most powerful way to do this is to prime your-self to start rolling forward when stuck.

Believe that it will work. Your belief will help get you unstuck. Your confidence, or even hope, that you are free to choose will get you moving because moving will feel easier. And when you freely choose to enjoy that free movement, you will find joy and power.

To see how this is possible, let's examine a very sim-ple task with two different outcomes and explanations of goals.

When people are asked to write a letter full of positive memories and emotions to a loved one, and then are asked how much they value the goal of maintaining that relationship, they say it is hugely important, and worth real, long-term investment.

But something surprising happens when people are asked to spend the same amount of effort writing a letter full of negative memories and emotions to a loved one – they say that the goal of maintaining the relationship is less important to them.

So what is happening? Somehow the mood energy from the activity changes the way they see their goal. Many traditional theories describe goals in a very rational way. They assume that people give a fixed value for their importance that is independent of the work involved in achieving that goal. And yet people's perception of how much they want something can be changed by how enjoyable the path to the thing will be. The means is valued as part of the ends.

So, if the work towards a goal is experienced as enjoyable, your appetite and energy for moving forward is increased rather than decreased.

When people were asked to set three goals that were important to their success throughout the course of a year, they were also asked to what extent they felt their goals were freely chosen. Was this something they wanted to do, rather than something that they felt they should be doing? Were these goals a natural reflection of their own internal values, or something they felt begrudgingly obliged to do?

They were asked throughout the year how hard, or easy, it was proving to work at their goals. And at the end of the year the same people were asked how they had progressed against the goals, which were also independently assessed.

In a sense, the results were not surprising. Those who felt their goals were freely chosen enjoyed pursuing their goals much more, and achieved their goals much more often, than those who felt forced to pursue goals. Often the goals were shared by different people, but those who felt that they had freely chosen their goals reported that the work to accomplish them seemed easier, even though they had actually worked harder.

Think about it. The people who put in the most effort, in an objective sense, felt that their work was mostly effortless, in a subjective sense.

Letting natural mechanisms spring into action is part of the surprising power of a Nowist mindset. Finding harmonious movement, rather than damaging yourself by pushing too hard in the wrong direction, growing less flexible by sitting on the sidelines, or avoiding warm-up activity.

CHOOSE ONCE, KEEP ROLLING FORWARD

Making fewer choices makes it easier to keep rolling forward. Instead of stopping between actions to choose whether to continue, it's more effective to make one decision to take a series of connected actions. You move towards the most enjoyable means of accomplishing something, and you make the necessary chore into an entertaining joy.

Because making deliberate choices requires energy, you don't want to fall into a Thenist trap of making too many unnecessary choices, or letting those choices become more painful and energy-draining than necessary.

In a particularly insightful series of experiments, the energy costs of making an effortful choice were shown to reduce the energy you have available for doing other things. The mental effort of working through all available options and then making the choice left people with less energy. They had less energy for making other decisions, less energy for getting on with tasks, and less energy for overcoming challenges.

People were asked to make choices in a variety of ways, and then given challenges to see how much energy they had used up. In one variation, one group was asked to spend time completing a series of demanding choices between products, while the other group simply had to rate products without making a choice. Individuals from both groups were then ushered into a second room and presented with twenty small paper cups of an unpleasant mixture of vinegar, orange cordial and water.

The experimenter then announced that they would be paid for drinking the disgusting mixture, but that it was entirely up to them how many cups to drink. On average, those who had made no previous choices managed to drink nearly eight cups. Those who had exhausted their mental energy making choices could drink less than two cups of the ill-tasting concoction.

In another variation, half of the individuals completed a very similar set of choices while the other half made only comparisons. This time they were subsequently asked to hold one of their arms submerged under nearly freezing water for as long as possible. Again, on average, those who had made no previous energy-draining decisions managed to hold their arms in uncomfortably cold water for well over a minute. This was more than twice as long as individuals in the other group, who had less energy available.

There was also a further investigation in which students who used up their energy making choices about what to study in the next semester were less able to keep practising maths problems ahead of what they thought was an important test. Instead they were distracted into reading magazines and playing video games, both put there to test their self-control. This was not about ability, it was about the kind of energy needed to persist.

The researchers tried a similar thing by asking shoppers about how many choices they had made, and how much effort they had put into their choices. The next step was to ask those same shoppers to complete a series of simple maths problems. Again, those who had spent the most on energy-draining decisions finished the fewest tests. It was the same when students were asked to finish unsolvable puzzles: those who had made the most prior choices persisted for much less time than those who had made none.

Of even more value to us in our exploration of power is one last experiment in which a group of people who had made lots of choices and another group, who had made no choices, were placed in a new room and asked to watch a short video.

The whole thing was a set-up, with the video player rigged to malfunction and the real test being how long it would take the participant to alert the experimenter to the problem. People who had made no previous choices used their abundant energy to take the initiative after only a couple of minutes, yet those who had spent time making choices took, on average, over twice as long to move into action.

ONLY THE RIGHT PAIN GETS THE RIGHT GAIN

You will waste life energy if you make choices harder than they have to be. It's not lazy to skip unnecessary effort, it's smart. There is no immediate pain–gain relationship. It has to be the right kind of pain for the right kind of gain. And sometimes fluid movement rather than pain is the best way to find the joyful gains you seek. You can make your choices effortless by listening to your implicit self, by what your unconscious has already figured out, and then getting to work.

'Only the right pain gets the right gain.'

BLOOD, GUTS AND GARAGES

Slowed down by a Thenist mindset, someone may wish very much that the world was better, but waste time thinking about decisions past, present and future. Talent remains untested and untried. The genie of action trapped in its bottle. Time spent waiting for the perfect time, the kind benefactor, the lottery win, the voice of Oprah or a time-travelling member of the Nobel Prize Committee to reassure you that this is the path, the choice, the idea, the journey that will make your effort worthwhile.

But making things happen is about exactly that – someone, somewhere, taking what they have and making something better. It doesn't have to be dramatic, or praised, or lead to prizes or the cover of *Time* magazine; but making things happen, joyously living despite, and because of, what happens to you, moving, testing yourself and loving the thrill of the thing – that's available. The power to just move forward.

YOU'RE GOING TO GET HIT, WHAT NEXT?

Most days you will get knocked back. There will be a surprise or a shock. Something unplanned – both welcome and unwelcome, serious or trivial.

Boxers get punched. Martial artists get punched, kicked, thrown and put in strangleholds. And because they know that they'll be hit, the best fighters get prepared for the impact, so they can respond smoothly when it happens.

In a study on kick-boxers it was found that the best professionals visualise the fight. They imagine the moment of impact – how they will feel and what they will do when the opposing force smashes into an unprotected nose or stomach.

They also imagine how their future self might respond to an attack in a way that minimises the impact. Boxers keep their guard up, move their heads from side to side. When the punch comes, they anticipate, stepping to one side, attempting to slip past the attack. Martial artists also step to the side, often blocking in one fluid movement before returning the force of the attack.

When smart boxers are hit they try to minimise the blow by moving away or with the punch. They might lean forward, smothering their opponent's arms. If close enough, they might allow the ropes to absorb some of the force by leaning back. And then springing back, returning the energy in their own counter-attack.

When thrown by an opponent, mixed martial artists attempt to roll away from the worst of the impact. The best tend to protect their head, often with both hands, as they roll. They tuck in their chin, breathing out, staying supple, avoiding their bones driving into hard ground and then smoothly roll up to their feet.

The most effective boxers and martial artists are attacked with the same ferocity as less effective fighters. The force behind the attack is just as strong, but they are able to think differently about the attack. And they react differently to the impact, using its power.

In a similar way, Nowists experience the same objective change as other people, but are much more able to smoothly adapt to it.

Psychologists in Rome[64] tracked how people in four different organisations responded to significant changes in their working lives. Some were nurses, whose roles were moving from being a traditional kind of doctor's assistant to becoming a modern, independent health-care professional. There were also postal workers, soldiers and lawyers. All were, like the nurses, having to change the way they worked.

All the groups were assessed to see whether they had a Nowist or a Thenist mindset, and then for how they coped with these big changes, which really had a major day-to-day impact on what they did and how they did it. On a percentage scale, their roles had on average experienced a transformation of 90 per cent.

It turned out that the Nowists embraced the changes and were much quicker to welcome them as an inter-esting new reality. This new reality was different, and 'at least different isn't boring', which they considered to be a good thing. From both experience and instinct Nowists sense that new realities offer them new oppor-tunities. The flux allows them to slide into new work and new experiences.

Since they're faster at embracing change, the Nowists have a head start on their Thenist colleagues, who are still debating, often with themselves.

Thenists argue about whether the past was better, or whether the future will be worse. They often spend valuable energy – and time – and waste the patience of others on going nowhere. This results in a lack of effective action that can benefit from, influence or even stop the changes.

Nowists put their effort into figuring out how to effortlessly make the most of the new situation – as it is. And so, instead of depressing themselves with unhappy, passive thoughts about their environment, they are turning that environment into their playground.

Think of individuals who practise parkour – they have developed a high level of reactive, Nowist thinking and an approach to moving effortlessly in their urban environment. Each concrete barrier, each steel railing, every brick wall or chain link fence represents an opportunity for proving yourself against a new challenge.

The parkour philosophy has origins in the experiences of Raymond Belle, the son of a French doctor who ended up in a military orphanage in Vietnam at only seven years old. Instead of becoming a victim of what was a harsh environment, he would sneak out at night to train on a military obstacle course – known as a *parcours* in French. Much later, in France, Raymond related his adventures to his hyperactive son, David, who started training in a similar way, but this time using the urban environment as his living obstacle course.

David's powerful energy attracted a group of friends, who together developed an approach sometimes described as *l'art du déplacement* – or the art of movement. Their aim is to move as smoothly as possible over obstacles, mastering each movement through repetition. The results were breathtaking for the millions who watched with amazement at videos of the group making impossible jumps across tower blocks and bridges. Individuals who practise parkour enjoy the implicit pleasure in movement and self-expression.

When there is freedom in obstacles, and joy in fear, the obstacle is welcomed, the fear embraced.

INVESTING EFFORT FOR EFFORTLESS ACTION

When a Nowist approaches an obstacle, they will often have already anticipated it. They may be specifically looking for an obstacle because they want a challenge, or because they know that the obstacle could slow them down. They practise their art of moving past obstacles – rolling with the punches. Some of this is actively preparing for the unplannable, but they are also very engaged in preparing for commonplace obstacles, the stuff of life, and things that that they know affect their lives in particular. It is the realisation of another surprising paradox about Nowists: Effort for Effortless.

When moving at speed, the fast-moving Nowist makes a lot of effort but does so to allow them to move effortlessly. They want to grow. First, by extending their own power to make things happen: their know-how, their know-how-to-do and their know-how-to-keep-moving.

An illustration of this was a study comparing expert, intermediate and novice players of Gaelic football. All the players were introduced to a new skill, and videoed to see how they responded.

The expert players watched the demonstration and then practised much more intensely than the intermediate or novice players.

What was striking was the performance of the players when tested months afterwards. The intermediate and novice players struggled to remember or demonstrate the new skill. But for the expert players, the new skill had become part of an easily remembered repertoire of effortless actions.

To achieve this kind of permanent effortless action requires self-coaching, the kind of self-talk and self-leadership that we've already discussed. Another method is to find people who can provide answers, perspectives and energy that we don't possess ourselves: to ask them questions, to watch and learn from them, and to recruit them to our cause – to have them actively engaged in revealing what we want to become.

THE MICHELANGELO EFFECT

This process of becoming has been labelled the Michelangelo Effect, because of his view that the best sculptors simply reveal what is hidden inside the stone.

But what kind of mindset would be most effective at revealing the self you want to become? To find out, psychologists recruited two hundred newly-formed couples, fresh and in love.[65] They asked them a bunch of questions including assessing them for Nowist and Thenist attitudes.

Over six months, they interviewed the couples and continued asking them insightfully designed questions about their partners' support for their practical and more existential strivings. It was found that high locomotors offered more welcome support, and insights, than high assessors. And that, in turn, high locomotors were much more open to suggestions and insights.

The couples who viewed change as a natural part of life, and were actively seeking psychological movement, found it enjoyable to give and take advice and insights.

Part of this appears to be because of the clarity of the suggestions that come from Nowists. They think to act – and so think in terms of things that are doable. They act to move – and are, as a result, life companions who take pleasure in sharing joy in the journey.

WHY PEOPLE LIKE TO FOLLOW SUPER-NOWISTS

It is easier to follow a person who is ahead of you. Particularly those who make following the path seem so very worthwhile, and especially if they're having fun, seem powerful and empowered, and are speeding along in a way that invites others to enjoy the slipstream.

Even when the person is not otherwise easy to get on with or easy to like, it is often more natural to be led by those who are leading the way.

Steve Jobs was a disagreeable genius. He shouted, he berated, he bullied, he could be harsh, unforgiving and irascible. But the impossible boss with the impossible standards, and attendant reality distortion field was also a force of nature. He created and sustained a feeling of purpose and movement. And his energy could sustain and inspire those who followed.

And this action–power, power–action spiral works both ways, as a highly original series of experiments demonstrated. They showed, time and again, that if you make someone believe that they are the formal leader of a group, that person will be more likely to take action.

In one experiment a group was divided into two halves. One half of the individuals in the group were taken aside and told they had been selected as leaders on the basis of having completed an aptitude assessment. They were assigned a Lego-building task, and given complete authority to direct how it was constructed, to assess how well group members had done, and to give out rewards to the group. The other half were taken aside and told that based on the aptitude test they would have no power and had to follow whatever the leader instructed.

This was all the clever set-up for what happened next. Each participant was asked to sit down in a divided cubicle to complete another kind of test – a computerised version of the gambling game blackjack (in which the aim is to get as close as possible to a total of 21 without going over 21). Each participant thought the game was genuine but it was in fact rigged. Each player received two cards totalling 16 and had to decide whether to say no or yes to another card.

People who felt powerful were significantly more likely to take action than those in the subordinate roles who felt powerless. Ninety-two per cent of those feeling powerful took the extra card, while only about half of those who felt lower power did the same. A sense of power made action easier.

But would a sense of increased power also make people more likely to act in a real-life situation? To test this out, they primed half of a group to feel less powerful by remembering a time someone had possessed power over them, and the other half to feel powerful by thinking back to a time when they had the power over someone else.

The next part of this sneaky experiment involved putting them into another room to complete a test. A fan was left on the desk next to theirs in a place where it blew air uncomfortably into their faces.

This time, people who were feeling powerful were more than twice as likely to move the fan than they were to ignore it, compared to less than half of those who were feeling less powerful.[66] The same is true for most situations: when you feel powerful, you are more likely to take action.

FROM ACTION TO GROWING INFLUENCE

As these experiments demonstrate, moving will make

you feel more powerful, which in turn will encourage you to take more action – which if successful will make you feel *even more* powerful.

This first action–power spiral can extend in a number of ways. One of these is that if you are seen to move powerfully and purposefully, you are more likely to gain influence.

This influence may be thought of as a form of gravity, and is also likely to move the actions of others. You may acquire resources, from your own work, and attract the support of others who can help you to keep moving further and faster.

Another young billionaire, Frank Wang, was also difficult to work with, so much so that his start-up team all quit within the first twelve months. But he soon created a level of energy – power – that attracted new employees to replace them. His company has a 70 per cent share of the fast-growing market for remote-controlled flying drones – delightful multi-winged mechanical marvels.

The lesson is not that you need to be a billionaire to attract the supportive actions of others, but that the act of moving forward has innate power. One action in a single moment contains power. And a continual stream of actions over time can be very powerful at influencing and attracting others.

At the simplest level, this means that many

people will interpret taking action as a sign of possessing power. For example, in one experiment putting your feet up on the desk was seen as a sign that you're able to take convention-busting action, and are therefore powerful. Other studies have shown that appearing to be immune to anxiety, or to concern about rejection, signal that someone is powerful – or at least powerful in the sense that you're able to defy conventions.

Similar conclusions were reached in another study. People were asked to read two different speeches from US presidents and then asked how powerful the speech made the president appear. Presidents who gave speeches that focused on assessment and deliberation were viewed as less powerful. When they emphasised moving forward, and taking immediate action, they were viewed as much more powerful. Even in little things, the person taking action can project a certain kind of power. And this makes sense – someone who has moved forward to action is putting their power into action rather than using up their energy for inaction.

Remember how feelings of power increased people's willingness to take action when an annoying fan was blowing air towards them? Well, when a video of a woman turning off an irritating fan was shown to people, they concluded that she was much more powerful if she turned off the fan than if she didn't turn off the fan. They even assumed that she was higher up in the hierarchy if she took action. Think about that. If you feel powerful, you are more likely take action, and if you take action, you are more likely to be seen as powerful.

WHO WILL HELP ME GO FASTEST?

The truth is that Nowists will tend to judge who to follow not so much on the basis of formal authority, or style, or structure, but on whether that leader gives them the opportunity to keep taking effortless action. They'll prefer a fairly traditional hierarchy when it allows them to move quickly. Or a no-rules, no-leaders culture when that works best for speed.

Nowists look for excitement, to test themselves, to go faster. You'll find them gravitating to emergency medicine, the military, activism, space exploration or the newsroom. It's not the organisation, it's the opportunity. So if you want to attract and benefit from that Nowist ability to look while leaping, the best way is to create opportunities for them to move rapidly. And push their limits.

That's why a firm like Valve Corporation, the creator of several ground-breaking video games, believes in a different way of working. In principle, anyone can work on any project they want. And new projects can be created by anyone who can get other people to work on their project. They even have desks with wheels so they can roll towards other people to form teams. It is spontaneous order in action. And all without the waste of fixed management structures and rules.

There's a lot for Nowists to like in this kind of set-up, but only when it doesn't stop their perpetual motion. So the trick is to tweak any organisational climate to make actions and decisions more effortless, and less painful. Nowists are better when they are able to see the negotiation process as part of the natural way of things, part of the change that they love. Then it stops being something to avoid, and starts being part of something they embrace. And when you work with other Nowists, the aim becomes taking the next step forward, rather than finding the perfect answer before you get started.

As a result, you may attract Nowists who want leaders who can speed up change. The preference is based not so much on leadership style, but on the speed of action that particular leaders make possible. It's a surprisingly powerful sequence of action–power spirals that increases the likelihood that more action will be taken, because you are feeling powerful in an action-oriented way. And fellow Nowists want to work with you because you make it easier for them to keep moving forward.

NURTURE THE POWER OF OTHERS

Embrace the power of others, and start to think of nurturing their power as something you want. When you want something as a Nowist, you tend to rapidly assess each situation for ways to get to your goal. As soon as you embrace empowering, and collaborating with, others, you will find it easier to naturally find joy in those activities.

Make it obvious that you are actively seeking the help of others. The evidence is clear: people want to know that you are open to their ideas, warnings and suggestions. They need to know that you are willing to be corrected, and what kind of help you need. And the faster you are moving, the more worthwhile it is to figure out how you can collaborate at speed.

And remember that reminding others of occasions when they were powerful, or moved fast, makes them more likely to feel and act in a Nowist way. And so it is worth your while investing the time to increase the power–action orientation of others. This in turn makes it more likely that you can get things done, and keep moving effortlessly forward.

past

when you
remember
feeling
powerful

#

action
becomes a
powerful
habit

future

CHAPTER 5
FINDING JOY IN YOUR NOW

There are three approaches psychologists like to use to figure out your level of happiness.

The first is to ask you about different aspects of how you think – they might ask whether you feel self-confident or well-adjusted. It is important stuff, but still a kind of tick-box happiness – even if you tick all of the boxes, and should therefore theoretically feel happy, you may not feel so in practice. This is another Thenist trap. You can become stuck, working hard while not getting as much in-life pleasure as you had imagined from your on-paper accomplishments.

The second way is to simply add up all the times you've felt good or bad over a period of time and figure out whether your highs outnumber your lows. This is a tally-up approach – generally, if you're ahead on good times, you will actually feel like you're having a good life.

It's the kind of happiness that you'd expect Nowists to experience, because they are busy enjoying what they choose to do, and choosing to do what they enjoy.

In one study it was found that Swedish high-school students with a Thenist mindset were more likely to be self-destructive, and experience more negative emotions. And those with a more Nowist mindset were more likely to experience more positive emotions, and more self-fulfilment.

A third way of measuring happiness is to ask how happy you are with your past choices, your present situation and with your prospects for the future. Questions like, if you could live your past again, would you change anything? And, is there anything you want to change about your present or future life?

In one study using this measurement of happiness, students with a Thenist mindset tried to protect themselves from disappointment and failure. Unfortunately, their efforts to protect themselves also deprived them of some of the best things in life – the delightful surprises, the stimulation that comes with uncertain progress and the satisfaction of overcoming challenges.

And, again, the influence of the Nowist mindset was to tip people towards moving actively towards a future that they valued via joyful experiences in the now. They took action that naturally led to what researchers described as 'spirals of empowerment'. They could look ahead far enough to see what they wanted, a kind of imaginative prophecy, and then take self-fulfilling actions to happiness.

FROM BASICS TO BOARDING

Once you master the basic leap into action, you can apply it to new situations and goals. Like anything else it's a progression, with one technique or fundamental skill opening up new possibilities.

The difference for people with a Nowist's mindset is that they actively seek out new moves and new combinations of those moves. They don't waste their lives wishing that they had, or regretting that they hadn't, or fearing that they might fail or be criticised.

Falling is moving, and moving is more interesting than experiencing nothing new.

Everything is made of something, and every accomplishment is made of actions, each making the next possible. In the 1940s, many different people, often surfers looking for a thrill when the surf wasn't up, started attaching rollerskates to boards. They called their new activity sidewalk surfing; the world would call it skateboarding.

This was all pretty one-dimensional: standing on a skateboard, using one foot to propel yourself forward, and avoiding obstacles. Opposition came from naysayers who worried about what might go wrong, and how much fun the kids seemed to be having, but the skateboarders kept moving and eventually developed two-dimensional tricks.

Frank Nasworthy was just a student in California who noticed the skateboarders rolling past, and happened to have seen polyurethane wheels in a factory owned by a family friend. He quickly fixed the wheels onto a standard frame, and gave the upgrade to some boarders who found that they could jump in new, previously impossible, ways. The new wheels meant that jumping didn't make the board slide out from under you. Frank sold 300,000 in a year, and boarders shifted tricks into three dimensions.

There were the Z-Boys, a legendary team of skateboarders who were among the first to start skateboarding in swimming pools, empty because of a drought. Skating the vertical walls as if they were waves, jumping high above the edge of the pool, their 'vert' style caught on, winning competitions and fans worldwide.

One can learn much about Nowists by studying the perpetual need to move that led to sidewalk surfing, the joy in spontaneous adventure that led to the dramatic vertical jumps of the Z-Boys, the everyday backyard experimentation that led to the 'Ollie' and the millions who have followed all the original pioneers.

They did it for fun. That's what Peggy Oki, one of the original Z-Boys, said. She's still a skateboarder and also an active campaigner for clean oceans. 'Everything I do, I choose because it's for fun.' And they did it for the freedom. The exhilarating, empowering energy that confirms that you have the power to take the risk and just go for it, which is part of the reason that Nowists get stronger, and feel right; rather than getting stuck wanting to be right or look right, they want that inner joy.

When someone wants to be right, they may focus on finding the answers that are viewed by others as correct, the one true way. They may even start to doubt themselves when they do feel right.

In one experiment, when people were put into a negotiation setting it was the Thenists who second-guessed themselves away from the best position. They felt less confident when the evidence suggested that they should feel more confident, and this was not because they didn't feel right. It was because they were suspicious of the feeling of feeling right. And when this is true in life more generally, such a mindset can move us away from the well-being of feeling right and the guidance such feelings gives us in relation to taking effortless actions and decisions.

A desire to look right, to look good, rather than feeling right inside, can also encourage various forms of cheating. So, when exercising, people wanting to look good might skimp on the part of the exercise that does most good to their bodies. When doing a push-up they may use the trick of 'sagging', lowering their stomach to the ground, or 'bouncing' off the ground to get a boost on the way up.[67] Instead of doing fewer repetitions with full movement, it can be tempting to do more repetitions while cheating.

The external audience may only be in your mind, it might be your future self, or someone specific who you fear or want to impress. Or, worse, sometimes you feel the judgement of a very general audience with very vague and unhelpful opinions.

Researchers at the University of Waterloo in Canada showed photos of important authority figures to people who were about to complete a task. They showed the photos so fast that participants wouldn't have been able to consciously register that they had seen the image. Some people were shown a photo with a smiling face, others a photo with a disapproving expression. The results were clear. The people who were shown the disapproving face performed worse in a reaction-time test than those who had seen the smiling face, and seemed to worry more in tests that were about moral judgements.[68] When their subconscious detected a disapproving audience, it nudged them towards a more Thenist mindset.

This desire to be right, and to look right, can lead to a winner-loses-all situation where everything that feels right is put aside for a dubious victory.

In that mindset, people may worry too much about the end rather than the means. So a fast athlete who wants to go faster takes banned performance-enhancing drugs. A cyclist wants to win more often, or just keep up with the rest of the peloton while expending less effort, and gets into swapping out his old blood for new, or even installing micro-engines in the bike frame to get that extra mile an hour.

The cheating has come from worrying about the external audience, and that same worry will plague them as they start to feel that they are pretending, or even faking, which they now are.

Something a little similar can happen with people who are very committed to being right and miss out on the best elements of *feeling* right. High-school students who worry a lot may miss out on the fun parts of being a student. And this includes enjoying studying. If you can do this it makes the task seem easier, which, in turn, reduces the energy needed to keep studying, leading to more effective study or simply a more harmonious, joyous life. Or both.

In a Nowist mindset it seems better to enjoy the moment while doing something that you value than to do something just to impress other people. And this leads to some curious, surprising moments of clarity and enlightenment: if work can be enjoyed, then it doesn't need to be avoided. And if enjoyment is included as part of your valued goals, then joy is not a distraction.

If enjoyment is not included, more or less harmoniously, as part of the valued goals then there are some kinds of effort that will not be made, just as there are some kinds of insights that cannot be reached, and opportunities that cannot be made to happen.

You won't tend to get the full benefit from the biceps curl without the full movement of the biceps curl, or the full thrill of the win without winning without cheating.

TOO FAST FOR SCHOOL, JUST FAST ENOUGH FOR LIFE

Those who excel when working towards goals they have been given, with predefined means and ends, may struggle to achieve much outside of such prescriptive environments. This is because they don't get to test their ability to choose their own goals or experience the growth that comes from the challenge of uncertainty. For less experienced Nowists, the need for speed and movement can work against them in academic environments, where they may struggle to slow down enough to explain themselves or please their teachers. They may even be written off as difficult, misdiagnosed as hyperactive, or criticised for being disinterested and unengaged.[69]

Some people are driven to find joy in adventure, while others are fortunate enough when growing up to have the kind of experiences that let them feel their strength without being overwhelmed. But the first time many of us realise that we can thrive when facing a challenge is when life throws up something unwelcome, even terrifying, that we aren't able to avoid.

Increasingly there is evidence of very significant differences in how people respond to stress and trauma. One team of researchers interviewed people who had been in or very near the 9/11 attacks in New York City. These people, described as high-exposure survivors, had followed a number of broadly different journeys, or trajectories, following their experiences of the day's events.[70]

One group had already been experiencing high stress leading up to 9/11, which got even worse and stayed that way for years afterwards. The other groups had not been experiencing much stress until the attacks. For some of these people, distress became very high immediately and only very gradually decreased; for others the distress was not that high immediately but increased in a delayed reaction. Another group responded with less distress, then gradually recovered, while a fifth group was able to remain stable under stress and maintain resilience both during and after the attacks.

The results revealed that not everyone has the same response to stressful events, whether that is a terrorist attack, the loss of a loved one, illness or a relationship breakdown. Nowists are able to move forwards using their own resources, their own way of dealing with stress and their own strategies for smoothly coping. These were not repressed people hiding their damage, but people who had the capacity to process or bypass the potential trauma of an external shock.

Even more startling is work by Stephen Joseph, a pioneering trauma psychologist, who had started his research more than a decade before 9/11. He found, completely to his surprise, that not only were some people more resilient than others but that about half of all those who experience extreme events, including explosions, shipwrecks, the death of loved ones and deep loss, end up reporting personal growth as a result.

Joseph's post-traumatic-growth people were also often surprised to find that they were able to transform the energy from an unwelcome shock into what felt like a better self, or at least a self that was on a journey;

EMBRACE THE PERPETUAL JOY OF MOVING PERPETUALLY FORWARD

either on a new path that included growth or an accelerated path to growth.

Resilience is generally better than non-resilience but it has its limits. You'll get back to being the same person you were before the trauma, but you may miss out on valuable opportunities for growth. By bouncing back while hardly missing a step, you may not notice that the situation contains useful signals, or the chance to propel yourself forward.

Most people experience both negative and positive changes in outlook after being exposed to trauma, but some tip towards movement, and as a result move upwards to growth.

Some of this growth is about personal changes, some is philosophical, and some is about changes in relationships. In a questionnaire developed to check on people's progress, three questions addressed the beliefs and behaviours linked to the emergence of post-traumatic growth.

- Are you open to new experiences?
- Are you always seeking to learn?
- Are you hopeful about your future and looking forward to new possibilities?

In all these the Nowist mindset is helpful since you are more likely to be open to new experiences, seeking to learn, and hopeful about your future.

Nowists seek change alongside movement and, as a result, will often find themselves in better places when they are hit by unanticipated events. They do not merely cope, they re-scope what is possible. Like comic book superheroes, bitten by spiders or bathed in radioactivity, they transform.

For Joseph, a key message is that growth is a journey, and it is here, again, that a Nowist mindset helps. He argues that stress brings about certain kinds of growth because it is this destructive level of power that unexpectedly transforms the person, their philosophy and their patterns of living. The Nowist expects, and seeks out, the unexpected. They want to be remade, and actively push towards transformative can't-go-back experiences.

In this way, you instinctively value changes that occur in your life, often as they are happening. And you express changes in your *perspective* through taking action to change your *life*. All of these are steps recommended by Joseph. Some people must learn to take them, and must sometimes painfully become 'active agents in their own lives' but Nowists are already active and leap, often with humour and joy, towards the growth to be found in challenges.

This humour and joy was seen in the attitude of an aid worker when he was unexpectedly imprisoned in

Iran. When asked how he survived twenty-eight days of solitary confinement he explained:

> By the end, I was doing 1,500 sit-ups and 400 push-ups a day. I told myself, I'm going to do a really long workout from breakfast until dinner, and my being here is the second part.

He went on to say that he found messages scratched into the walls in Farsi saying 'You can get through this,' 'Don't ever give up,' and 'Nobody stays here for ever.'

All of these were messages of hope and movement – many from previous political prisoners, alone in a cell, extending their #Now beyond the present moment to a future where they would be free. They were able to imagine another person who would need encouragement. Former inmates reached mentally beyond imprisonment towards hope for eventual freedom, and beyond fear to action in the present.

By the time the aid worker was released he was over thirty thousand sit-ups and twelve thousand push-ups ahead of most of us. And he was still laughing. People like him look for growth and adventure. They have often been adventuring their whole lives, so are not easily overwhelmed when unexpected shocks arrive. Even when those are as dramatic and awful as imprisonment in a foreign country.

This is in part because the adventuring tendencies of a Nowist are joined by an enjoyment of their own nature. People in a Nowist mindset tend to challenge themselves to see what impressive feats they can manage, and love the whole experience, even if they fail. Sometimes the whole thing is funnier and more memorable if they don't succeed.

A FEISTY SPIRIT OF SURVIVORSHIP

This laughing-is-winning approach can develop what some researchers called a 'feisty spirit of survivorship', which you can cultivate even before you are faced with extreme challenges. It is also something that can be developed deliberately by some people facing new stresses, including those that are life-threatening.

The phrase 'feisty spirit of survivorship' was used to describe one of the strategies adopted by cancer survivors who took part in a dragon boat race championship. The teams were put together to provide survivors with an opportunity for social support and for the kind of psycho-physical benefits that come from movement. You feel stronger by using your strength. You feel more able to move on because you are moving more.

Dragon boat racing goes back over two and a half thousand years to competitions between fishing villages along the Yangtze River in China. They symbolised the re-energising of the dragon, which brought new growth to the rice fields. Modern dragon boats are often constructed of fibreglass yet are still made in the shape of a dragon, and in many ways still represent growth and power: twenty paddlers work together as the drummer provides a heartbeat, and a cox provides eyes to see the way across 500 yards of water.

Symbolically, taking part in a new activity just for people who had experienced cancer signalled to participants that cancer had somehow opened a new opportunity. As one person said, 'If I hadn't had my breast cancer, I wouldn't even know about the team.' The after-cancer life tally sheet has a positive entry that could not have been made before the disease struck. And the same can be true for other challenges and setbacks. Each can be used as a marker, after which specific new adventures are experienced and celebrated.[71]

There were some participants who exhibited a notably 'let's get moving' mentality. They were described as superwomen by others who took part, yet it appeared it was rather that they possessed a different mindset, one that could be adopted by others facing similar stresses. One of the differences between them and the others was that they embraced the energy potential of a life-changing event and transformed it – using it as fuel for further growth in their work and home lives, and as a reminder to provoke continual movement.

This transformative ability to make good things happen is a quality you can discover in yourself. And psychologists are discovering something about those Nowist mindsets that can move past being stuck or broken and slide smoothly, or relatively smoothly, into growth. Their defining characteristic isn't neutral contentment, it is joy.

EXPECTING TO MAKE GOOD THINGS HAPPEN

It is good to expect good things to happen. This kind of classic optimism has been shown to open people up to more positive interpretations of events and make them more likely to hope for positive experiences in the future.

Athletes who expect good things to happen are more likely to experience enjoyment in movement for its own sake.[72] They are more likely to enjoy being carried away in the motion and speed of their sport, because they are not interrupting their enjoyment with negative thoughts.

And, again, this is a good thing, yet the difference is that an athlete with a Nowist mindset enjoys the movement and *expects* to make more good things happen. They are looking for ways to fill the future with more of the change and movement that turns them on, and they also tend to turn the pursuit of what they want into part of the fun challenge.

They view what happens as something they can influence, and even more crucially for the Nowist this positive sense of influence means that they make changes in the only place and time that change can happen, the present.

So, instead of getting stuck regretting the past, fearing the future, or being paralysed by trying to find the perfect plan, successful happy people actively change the future by taking action today. They don't spend time figuring out the one most important thing. Instead, they instinctively do the next positive thing. They keep moving. They look while leaping, and leap while looking. They don't get hung up on getting everything right, but on making a start, and making things happen.

When high school students were asked by psychologists at the University of California about how they viewed the relative importance of the past, present and future, there was a clear link between accomplishments and a present-future focus (where they focused more on the present and future than the past).[73] Those Nowists with a present-future focus were also more likely to have higher self-esteem than those who focused equally on all areas of time, while those who looked backwards, comparing their current circumstances to the past or agonising over what they wish could be changed in the past, had a much lower self-image.

And those who were happier and accomplished more tended to be able to see the way in which past, present and future are interconnected. They were more able to believe that they could make good things happen because they could see how to make good things happen. They had an ingrained confidence, often a practical been-there-changed-that confidence that made those positive expectations actively, rather than passively or naively, optimistic.[74]

SLIDING PAST DOWNERS, HURDLING OVER OBSTACLES

This kind of Nowist confidence is increased by actively testing yourself against your limits. In this way, you discover your own strength to overcome and this quality is developed further.

Those in a Thenist mindset tend to avoid challenges with uncertain outcomes, and situations that include anti-goals, things they fear, dislike or want to prevent happening.

When something bad does happen, the negative emotions can trap them in the past, and the way that makes them feel can stop them being able to take action to improve anything.[75] Often, it's not that they have forgotten how to take action, it's just that they are so weighed down by past emotions that they have no energy for the present, or available mind space for the future.

When in this spiral of negativity, our sense of #Now becomes distorted. The negative past dominates our thoughts, and we become cut off from both the present and the future.

When thinking this way, people are unlikely to enjoy the present or their own selves. They are less likely to look effectively for pleasure in the next challenge, or to succeed. They may drag themselves through what is necessary, and may even do it well, but they will have discarded the possibility of making better things happen, and missed out on the pleasures of doing and moving.

Feeling positive about the future also makes it easier for Nowists to better imagine practical next steps towards what is desirable. Once they are moving – or leaping – forward, they focus more on enablers – situations and events that enable – and less on blockers, things that make you slow down or stop you in your tracks.

In a hurdles race, Nowists see jumping hurdles as part of the fun, but people in a Thenist mindset focus on the pain of jumping. They see each hurdle as a chance to trip, fall or injure themselves in a humiliating, perhaps even career-ending, failure.

The Nowist looks at sequences, clearly seeing actions ahead of the race. They look at the race in terms of patterns and steps. Seven steps to the first hurdle. Three steps between each hurdle. Looking ahead as they leap.

COUNTERFACTUALS AND PREFACTUALS

The two mindsets also look at the past differently. Nowists cycle back into the past, but only for insights that help them cycle forward, faster or better – usually this means thinking about what you could do differently in the future based on the outcomes of your actions in the past. And not dwelling on the past if it drains energy from #Now.

People in a Thenist mindset, and those who feel powerless, or passive, tend to look back at what they cannot change. This might be the events of the past, which cannot be directly changed, or the actions of other people, outside of their control.

It's an important difference that uses the same ability. You can re-view the past or pre-view the future. You can emotionally time travel to re-experience or pre-experience.

Re-feeling can be very real, your body responds as

you re-live something that has happened. Or a feeling that you've experienced in the past. Our minds can reconfigure past sensations, and use those re-mixes to create possible future emotions.

You can also take lessons without the feelings, by thinking about the facts of an event or experience, and the sequence of causes and effects, actions and out-comes. We can learn from what has previously happened, or simply get stuck in what we like most or least about the past.

When you look backwards, it helps to focus on what you feel that helps you move joyfully forward. What did you love that moves you to keep moving? What did you do then, you personally, that you can do differently now? What about the past energises you, and lets you feel powerful in the #Now?

LIKING YOURSELF, AND BEING ON YOUR OWN SIDE

Just as background images of a disapproving face can slow you down, causing self-sabotaging second-guessing, so foreground images of your own approving self can help to speed you up.

Your positive self-regard can act as a cheerleader, not so much pretending that you are better than you are, but being impressed with your own efforts, and amused, informed or entertained by your mistakes and mishaps. It sounds simple, but it is nevertheless easy to forget the benefits of being good to yourself, ensuring that you are on your own side to make life and its pursuits worthwhile and fun.

One study about how people recover after injury showed how the ability to persist, to spiral upwards and forwards, can be wrongly thought of as imperviousness to negative emotion.[76] This is because it can be easy to form the impression that toughness is about the absence of sadness or disappointment, so people try to give the false impression that they are not sad, or angry, or worried, or disappointed.

Listen to the difference between two injured athletes as they describe what they do with their feelings:

> I talk to my friends about pretty much anything, so injury wasn't much different. When I was feeling down about my injury, they were the first people I spoke to . . .

> When you are playing sport you never want to show that you are weak. Talking is just not something I do. You just get on with it . . . Nobody has ever come up to talk to me about their emotions.

The first athlete scored higher for the kind of commitment that leads to faster recovery, but he does not confuse toughness with pretending not to have emotions. The second athlete scored lower on the kind of commitment that leads to faster recovery. Later, athletes also reported that the lack of an emotional outlet would mean that negative emotions would tend to build up and leave people like the second athlete moving between depression and anger.

Stress, or challenges, will not automatically lead to either bad outcomes or good outcomes. The difference is about the gap between difficulty and your ability, not too much or too little. So that you can be stretched or propelled willingly, allowing you to grow to meet the challenge[77].

The Nowist mindset is more likely to lead to a spiral of happiness because of its greater effectiveness in regulating the way you feel so that you can treat yourself kindly while still throwing yourself into situations that have an element of stress. When you know that disappointment is valuable, or a fall can create something exciting, or a setback is part of the journey, growth is likely.

Challenges are more likely to damage you when you don't know when to stop, and when the pain is not a part of a learning process. Demands are more likely to overwhelm you when you can't change to whatever perspective gives you the clearest view of where you are and what happens next.

When Olympic gold medallists were interviewed as part of research into the relationship between adversity and performance, there was a revealing pattern of belief.[78] They believed that experiencing adversity was absolutely necessary because it developed the skill to overcome and then use adversity for growth. This skill became part of their repertoire, available to transform the stresses of life, training and competition. And able to expand their view of what was possible since attempting something with adversity as part of the package was not something to be avoided.

The following was typical of their attitude:

If I hadn't failed in Athens, I wouldn't have succeeded in Beijing . . . It takes losses like that sometimes, even though they're hard to swallow, hard to deal with. It will benefit you later on in life. I just learned not to get so hyped up or worried about stuff.

Among the athletes who did not win medals there were some who had been picked for every team at every age. The downside to their relatively straight-forward earlier success was that they they didn't learn as much about their limits, or how to overcome them.

In the same way, there are people who are always top of the class, or the most popular, who fit what others are looking for, and make an effort to fit into whatever their peers see as safe and right. The problem with this is that you may end up being tamed too easily, and learn to accept limits on what you can really achieve or how you really want to live or work. Success guides you, rather than joy.

This is similar to the relationship between power, or a feeling of power, and taking action, but here the benefit is that coping with high demands increases your ability to cope gracefully with challenging circumstances.

And this, in turn, allows you to take pleasure in thriving and growing in demanding circumstances. Almost as if you were watching an action movie: cheering on the hero, feeling the pain as they run barefoot across glass, their exhilaration as they slip while scaling a skyscraper with suction pads, or their effortless fluidity as they battle against endless waves of henchmen.

When your action hero falls, or is beaten down, you know this is just one act in a story arc that is building towards more adventure.

And so it is when you adopt a Nowist perspective. You'll often be happier fighting the odds, stretching and expanding what is possible for you and your present situation.

In the change-hungry Nowist mindset, you lean towards the future. And you do it from an active, practical, let's-make-this-work view of the world.

If your life has taught you to be active and decisive, then you are more likely to make decisions and take action. Significant others can help – parents, teachers, friends, colleagues and managers – but you are also, and always, your own significant other. You see what you do, and you can talk yourself into paralysis or movement.

FASTER THAN SPEEDING STRESS

As this becomes natural, it can also become effortless, so that your intuitive response to stress or adversity is tipped towards action, growth, happiness and even joy.

In a test of this, people were placed into various kinds of stressful conditions, completing complex and often conflicting tasks under time pressure, then shown lists of negative, neutral and positive words.[79] They were asked to provide positive responses each time they saw negative words. The results showed that people with a Nowist mindset in a stressful situation were much faster to provide positive responses. Their performance actually improved, providing an advantage over other people.

In a similar way, they were faster to recognise happy faces in a crowd of angry faces.[80] And, remarkably, Nowists found themselves in a better mood when subliminally presented with angry faces so fast that they didn't know what they'd seen. In each case, the fast automatic thinking of Nowists had already lined up a positive approach to a negative event.

In these situations their need for action kicks in – it recognises the time-pressured, highly demanding situation. Some of this is because high demands are more interesting, and bring more thrills and happiness. And some of it is because those highly demanding situations tend to crush, paralyse or depress those in a Thenist mindset. Pressure and stress are things to avoid, but avoiding all demands can steal opportunities for growth. If you withdraw from what makes you uncomfortable, gradually your ability to cope will weaken. And you never get to enjoy your real power to transcend.

Instead, you may choose to take a more Nowist approach to developing your Nowist abilities. Start with progressively taking on higher demands, and embracing those demands as opportunities for growth. And not just as unwelcome but necessary growth, not as a list of challenges as chores, or obstacles as drudgery. If a job is worth doing, it's usually worth enjoying the job, or at least some part of the job.

JOY NOW, JOY TOMORROW

Finding pleasure in change, and joy in doing, has the potential to allow you to escape ultimately futile spirals.

You are able to free yourself from meeting other people's real or imagined expectations, or judging yourself against a level that always increases and does not deliver enjoyment, only the absence of disappointment.

As an example, let's look at the results of an experiment involving a group of people who were prone to excessive self-criticism. Its members were given either a three-week course of mindfulness meditation exercises, or a three-week course of practising positive emotions that included joy, hope, pride, serenity and amusement.[81]

After a month, both groups reported lower symptoms of depression, but only the group with the positive emotions had increased satisfaction with life. People who actively made themselves feel a broad range of positive emotions felt that their lives had improved in terms of meaning, pleasure and engagement with living.

This was surprising because, though it was expected that self-critics would respond most to mindfulness, the findings suggest that for some people, and in some situations, active experiences are more likely to move them forward. Nowists move beyond coping to an upwards spiral of growth.

this is your average
standard #now

this is your unhappily
stressed #now

this is your happily extended #now

CHAPTER 6
THREE STREAMS OF #NOW

Time. It's the same for everyone. Yet time is used and experienced very differently. Some people make time, others are crushed by it. You can stretch time, waste time, or invest time. Your minutes can seem like hours, or your months seem like days. Time can freeze, or we can feel frozen in time.

So far we've explored how people think, feel and act differently depending on their approaches to movement and change. We've looked at functional impulsivity, the ability of some people to make decisions faster than others but with better results. We've examined locomotion, the desire some people have to keep moving forward. And the ways these two abilities combine in the Nowist mindset to allow effortless action and decisions to work smoothly and fluently together.

In this chapter we'll look at how Nowists use, live with and think about time.

CONNECTING WITH #NOW

Not everyone sees time in the same way. Some people focus most on the past whilst others give their attention to the present. And there are some who are most interested in the future. Not everyone sees clear connections between how actions in the past have created the situation in the present, or how actions in the present will shape, or create, the future. They are isolated, disconnected and therefore cut off from the power of the #Now.

Some people, in a Thenist mindset, can make the connections, but they get stuck worrying about, or regretting, the gaps between what really happened and what they wish had happened. The same thing can happen when they consider the future: they see possible connections, but making those connections work seems too much effort, or too hard to imagine. It's a short step from here to a downward spiral of passivity – and can be recognised in common thoughts such as:

No idea how things turned out this way.
Not a clue where to go from here.

Nowists see the connections and the route to making them happen. The realisation of this helps to instil a sense of confidence and trust in the #Now, because it will propel them forward.

I can make good things happen.
If I take action a better future can be created.

Remembering positive feelings can show us clues as to how we might guide positive action in the present. If Nowists look backwards, it is to cheer themselves onward, or to learn more about whatever will help them to understand what they value and how to reach what they value more effectively.

Elite sportsmen rely on this sensation to enable them to compete at the highest level. For instance, imagine a skier who is competing in a multi-event competition. At this elite level each skier has the technique, ability and physicality to achieve success – the difference between the athletes comes with their ability to adapt to each event, to each course and, importantly, their ability to adapt their action to their goals.

When working their way down a moguls slope – the

competition with a variety of demanding mini-hills to navigate – the skier gains points for stunts, a certain amount for speed, and most of the points for the way they turn (not skidding on the snow, or ploughing, but using an aggressive, controlled technique). Whereas for the downhill skier it is the carving turns that enable them to keep control at a rapid pace. Speed skiing is about straight runs in which the first half of the course demands acceleration, followed by the middle 100 metres where the skiers are timed to see who is fastest, ending with the last 400 metres, where it is important to slow down before running out of room. Each event has its own timings and styles.

In snowboarding – whether the snowboarders are competing in speed or stunt events, which both demand particular techniques and jumps – the main goal of the sport is to reach new limits, discover new possibilities. The snowboarders love the thrill and rush of pushing boundaries as well as the enjoyment of being within a community of likeminded freedom lovers.

Most people, particularly the pioneers, get into something like snowboarding for the thing itself. They are driven by their passion for it and the need to move towards it.

Consider the way Shaun White became the golden boy of American winter sports. At the age of six Shaun's mother wanted her highly energetic son to slow down, burn more energy, and so encouraged him to go snow-boarding with his brother. 'Copy your brother,' she said, and, so the story goes, he was outperforming his seven-year-older sibling by the end of the day. 'Go back-wards,' she asked in another effort to slow him down, and he mastered reverse boarding, a skill that would eventually allow him to bring back a haul of medals.

Of course, Shaun has a natural talent on the snow but the powerful thing to remember is his irrepressible passion for movement and discovery – the passion that propels Nowists like Shaun White forward into a stream of actions.

It is much the same in very different avenues of life and work. People propelled by their joy in something are able to see the future clearly enough to connect their actions in the present to the future. They build streams of action that connect them to their passion.

YOU AND YOUR FUTURE NOW

Your ability to change what you do in the present based on what you want to happen in the future is a kind of action-oriented mental time travel that devel-ops from childhood to adulthood.

When people reach adulthood they have approxi-mately sixty thoughts about the future every day, or around four an hour. One of the few studies to

NOWISTS
MAKE
FRIENDS
WITH THEIR
KINDER
WISER
FUTURE-SELVES

measure what kind of future thoughts we have found that about half concern specific future events, while half are general musings regarding the future.[82]

We have fewer thoughts about the distant future, so close to 30 per cent of our thoughts focus on what is happening later the same day, and another 30 per cent on events in the next week. Then they drop sharply, with less than 20 per cent devoted to the next month, only 12 per cent regarding what is likely to happen up to a year away, and fewer than half a per cent focused beyond the decade.

People tend to have more positive than negative thoughts about the future, and thoughts about the more distant future are viewed as much more important. You think about relationships, your major goals, or how your life is going to be in the future. The really big questions.

Some of our thoughts are about how we anticipate feeling in the future, and some thoughts about the future change our feelings in the present. Fewer than ten a day, but they can be very important.

When a team of psychologists asked people to keep a record of their emotional future thinking, they found the most frequently anticipated feelings were joy or enthusiasm. And that people, on average, were more likely to be fearful about the future than to think they would feel fear when they reached the future. This can become a typical Thenist trap – to scare yourself with negative self-talk about future thoughts that are too general to be understood; and then keep that fear of the unknown bottled up, which leads you away from doing anything helpful.

The Nowist trick is to be more specific about visualising yourself in the future. As you understand the future better, and make it more like the present, you are able to more easily imagine what and how you'd make the future successful. And you are also able to take action in the present to be prepared for the future.

People who are closer to their future selves tend to choose actions in the present that will help them now *and* later. When the present-you is more in harmony with the future-you, you're able to let your intuitive reasoning make choices that you value and believe are worth pursuing.

And when you can really vividly picture the future-you doing future things, you can get a sense of what that means for you today and your actions today.

There is a greater feeling of confidence because you have an understanding of the deep gist of the thing, rather than just the surface dates or projected facts. This helps you to better plan steps towards whatever you value through the perspective of the future-you.

You'll feel less intimidated by what you don't know, or don't like, because the future feels real, and you already know how to deal with day-to-day reality.

You are more likely to think of yourself in the subjective first person when imagining yourself doing something in the near future. You feel like the same person in the present, the person doing the imagining, as you will be in the future. Along the lines of:

> I'm doing some shopping this afternoon.
> I'm seeing friends later today.
> I'm working on my project tomorrow.

You are more likely to think of yourself from a detached vantage point when imagining the distant future. Almost as if you are observing a person separate from yourself doing something in the future. Or a future without you being clearly identifiable. So you'll be more likely to think:

> In a few years, there'll be some changes.
> It's going to be a hot summer.
> Getting older will be different.

The useful thing about being able to travel temporarily into the future is that you can try to pre-feel and pre-view. And this gives the present-you the chance to plan, choose or prepare. If you can do that for longer jumps into the future, you can work backwards from the future to take longer sequences of actions, with much more powerful results. Some achievements are only possible, and worthwhile, when patterns of actions are connected together over years, decades or longer.

This is one of the paradoxical tensions of the power of #Now. Each moment of #Now has more power when it is connected to other moments of #Now. Nowists enjoy action *in* the present, and they take action that can move them forward now and in the future.

Nowists plan, not because of a love of planning but so that they can keep moving. In this way, they can enjoy the continual payoff of action and increase opportunities for task-juggling, stream-hopping and combining actions for multiple benefits.

They live according to a Nowist Law of Big Numbers by creating more chances to succeed. Because they try so many things, they are not surprised by how it feels to fail, and know how to respond. And because they have other streams of action, they accept the possibility of stuff not working out, and embrace the pleasure of making stuff work out in the end.

Whether your future self will move you to take positive action in the present depends on a few different things. It will depend on how much you feel that your desirable future self is possible. It will depend on how easy it is to imagine your future self, and how much control you feel over attaining your desired future.

As an example of this, a group of people were asked by psychologists about the characteristics of their possible future selves they most hoped for, and most feared.[83] They hoped for attributes like being successful, loving, caring, athletic, happy, calm, attractive, honest and outgoing. And they feared becoming things like ordinary, arrogant, alone, unemployed, homeless or stressed.

Next, people were asked to write about the future self they most feared becoming and the future self they most hoped to become. It was found that the future was much more likely to motivate action when you could bring the future self quickly to mind, found it easy to imagine and felt that you would have control over the situation.

A large factor in being able to 'see' the future self you want to become depends on whether you think people generally succeed or fail at whatever you're trying to do. This is highlighted by the fact that when the group in the study was reminded that failure is very common in a particular situation they were more motivated to take action when they thought about what they didn't want to become. And when people were reminded that success was very common in a particular situation, they were more easily moved to action by thinking about what they wanted to become.

If you believe that success is likely it's easier to motivate yourself by thinking about what you want to gain than what you might lose. If you're in a Nowist mindset, you tend to think you can find a way to make good things happen because you are focusing on the gains, which in turn naturally encourages you into action, and clearer work.

Even then, it can be valuable to flexibly switch between different kinds of motivation depending on whatever you feel is most likely to happen. Switching to avoiding loss, or failure, for just long enough to get you moving. And then switch back to a more gain-focused outlook as your movement makes success seem more likely.

COLLABORATIVE MINDSET

Whether your future self will move you to take positive action in the present depends on a few different things. It will depend on how much you feel that your desirable future self is possible. It will depend on how easy it is to imagine your future self, and how much control you feel over attaining your desired future.

So when Joichi Ito, director of the MIT Media Lab, wanted to find out what was happening in Japan after a magnitude 9 earthquake hit the country, he moved into action. The earthquake had provoked a tsunami that flooded a nuclear reactor and caused explosions. His family was there, and he wanted information about radiation levels, but news reports had none, nor could he find any publicly available data.

He did what seemed natural, transforming the shocking news and his desire to find out more into forward motion. He was shocked, and shock provided energy for the actions that followed. It could have overwhelmed him, it could have stopped him moving or spun him into an unhelpful orbit or direction, but he didn't let that happen.

Instead, he jumped onto the Internet, formed a loose working group with some like-minded people, and started to build a system for measuring radiation. Three years later, the energy of that personal moment of shock had created a worldwide community, who take radiation measurements and upload them onto a publicly accessible website.

Ito argues that in a very complex world it's best to keep things very simple. He says, 'It's about stopping this notion that you need to plan everything, you need to stock everything, and you need to be so prepared, and [instead] focus on being connected, always learning, fully aware and super-present.' He believes that is what a Nowist does.

The Nowist approach is not to take the most dramatic or risky approach. It is not generally about wild gambling or leaping in the dark. This is not crazy impulsive. Instead it creates space to think and does not delay taking a first positive step.

One of Joi's first actions was to overcome any lack of know-how by reaching out to a wider community of people and to use this community to gain knowledge and support and work collaboratively towards both his own goal and those of the rest of the community. The Nowist looks for those first, space-creating, energy-enhancing steps.

THREE STREAMS OF NOW

The ways our lives develop, especially in our modern world, mean that it is not possible to think about doing just one thing. Nowists go further, they embrace the fact that there are always so many things to do and enjoy. It is the ability to move between them that can increase our success, both in how we work and our happiness.

As you know, in this book, the # represents the moment of #Now where everything happens, the only point in time when you can take action. For me, an expanded # has also started to represent three streams of goals and actions.

Since we can't keep everything in mind all of the time, a guide that can be remembered easily is more useful for effortlessly moving between our various interests, actions, passions and goals.[84] There are many time-management systems and you may follow one of them. Nowists keep a strategic view – of what matters to them and what they are doing – in mind to guide effortless action.

To think more like a Nowist, a powerful start is to work with three streams of #Now – with the kind of things that matter most to you in each stream. It doesn't have to be three, but the number has been deliberately chosen to be adapted to our natural limits of working memory. Most people can only keep about four things in mind at any one time (whether concepts or groups of things), and so it made sense to keep the streams at three.

So there are three streams, and up to three active goals or actions in each stream. They will be flexible, because you won't always remember them and because priorities and circumstances change, but they provide a guide to keeping what you value in mind as you move forward.

The space between each horizontal line of the # can represent a sequence of actions towards an overall priority in your life or work. The vertical lines of the # create a sense of timescale related to particular goals or areas of your life or work.

When my son saw a printed version of the streams of #, he started to fill it in with the things that mattered most to him. My son chose home and family as his first stream, his second stream was about school and learning, and he described his third stream as being about friends and fun. He asked me to share what he'd written, along with his view that 'if a ten-year-old kid can understand it, anyone who reads your book can make it work'.

The power in such a Nowist approach to time and tasks is not that you always remember everything perfectly. Instead, the power comes from the improved outcomes that follow from viewing life as multiple streams of action. You will still need to plan out actions to achieve goals, but you'll be more likely to plan for goals that contribute to what really matters to you. This approach also helps you to keep what you love in mind, so that you can move towards what motivates you. And naturally move away what is not in harmony with what you love or need most.

You can also choose to pursue happiness and achievements that depends on your actions rather than passively depending on others. Instead of relying on events that are way outside your power to influence, you can work towards any objective, or dream, big or small, with what you have from where you are #Now.

The dream can be daunting, but again you can think backwards from it to actions that make the dream more likely. And you can work forwards to take those actions that put you in situations that make your dreams possible. If you want to be a movie director, then work out how to get yourself in the same room as people who work in the movie business. That might be college; it might be creating online videos; it might be taking a job of any kind in the entertainment industry; or networking your way into the company of friends of friends who can help.

If you want to be surrounded by friends and family all your life, and not be that person who is alone or friendless, then the same principles apply. Work backwards from what you love, and know what will matter to you over the long term. Imagine yourself in the first person, the real future-you. Feel what you'll feel. Think what you'll think. And then, with the wisdom that comes from making friends with future-you, work forwards from #Now.

The truth is that people who achieve good things, and have found joy throughout their lives, have much in common. You'll find that happy, successful people who profess to have never had a plan actually made planning part of their success. And that successful, happy people who claim to be focused on only one priority have juggled many priorities.

With three flexible streams of actions, you can move effortlessly between them. You can be happy to take time with your family because that's time that's precious, and won't come back. Or time on the beach or for dancing or reading, because life is for living. And time pursuing your work because you must provide for yourself. As a Nowist you will feel better when you are learning, useful and moving forward.

Seeing life as being about creatively connecting streams of action makes it easier to absorb the energy of unwelcome shocks or less dramatic setbacks. So that when you can't succeed the way you'd originally intended, you are able to slip into one of your other streams of action, or replace one method or means to an end with something quite different. And because you were already looking for better alternatives, you can find them.

Consider Kurt Yaeger. The Californian was already a professional BMX rider, and a part-time actor, and was studying as a masters student when his accident happened. He was forced to swerve to avoid a car and crashed his motorbike into a metal pole. The collision broke his back and pelvis, and damaged his left leg so badly that surgeons had to amputate it below the knee.

In the aftermath he considered killing himself. It wasn't just the leg, it was the pain, and the prospect of a painful rehabilitation ahead. But he remembers saying to himself that 'it was time to stand up and get better'. So he stood up and got better. It took thirty surgeries over four months to get out of the hospital. It took another year to rebuild his motorbike and perform his first wheelie. Then another couple of months to get back on a BMX.

IF LIFE
IS FAST
LIVE
FASTER

And, in a very Nowist way, he was able to jump between multiple action streams to keep moving forward. He tried sticking his prosthetic foot onto his bike's pedal with tape, velcro and eventually succeeded with clipless magnetic pedals that he invented in collaboration with his wider network. He became the world's top-ranked Adaptive BMXer. Online videos of him performing stunts one-footed attracted journalists. Their articles led to a music video for a UK band, Rudimental. His near-death experience was transformed into renewed efforts in his, previously part-time, acting career; hit movies followed, as did parts in big TV series. And he became an entrepreneur, turning his one-off magnetic pedal solution into a business.

Before his leg was amputated, he moved between multiple streams of action. BMX. Acting. University. After his loss, his past experiences helped. He knew how to get up from a painful fall and he knew how to grab hold of opportunities. Better BMX. Bigger Acting. New Business.

Nowists like to find ways of achieving multiple goals with one action. This is known as multi-finality.[85] They believe that there are usually many ways of accomplishing the same goal. This is known as equifinality. And they prefer not to choose ways of achieving one goal that block them accomplishing other goals. This is known as counter-finality. These beliefs and preferences naturally lead them to choose ways of working that create more freedom to make future choices. As a Nowist, because you are better at 'seeing' possible choices, you always have better choices.

And when your planned actions come together to create unplanned opportunities, you are able to spontaneously leap while looking. As a Nowist, you live and move in the joy of #Now.

TIME-STRETCHING

Some people prefer doing more than one thing at a time, they like the feeling of competence or the absence of boredom that they get from task-juggling. It's fun, effective, and it stretches time.

They may enjoy juggling micro-tasks such as answering an email while speaking to a partner while watching a movie or cooking an omelette. They may work in a similar manner too: choosing to move from task to task, or taking on more and more, maybe even more than is possible, so that there is always a stream of competing actions to juggle. This develops a situation where the main challenge is to be able to adapt to each new task – like life played as a game of Tetris, each task rotated in your mind so that it fits into your world.

Not everyone who likes task-juggling is naturally good at it. And not everyone who is really good at it says they like doing it. Some studies have shown an occasional gap between levels of enthusiasm for task-juggling and levels of competence at juggling those tasks.[86]

So people may like driving while using a phone, but be particularly dangerous because they are much worse at task-juggling than they think. This is a lot like Dickman's dysfunctional impulsives, people who make bad decisions because they find it hard to think clearly, or like to be reckless.

And it turns out that this is very different from the way people think who *are* able to effortlessly juggle tasks. They are much more like Dickman's functional impulsives, they task-juggle because they have task-juggling skills. And some of them are extraordinarily good at keeping balls in the air.

One team of psychologists put task-juggling to the test by getting people into a very realistic driving simulator and then calling the participants up on their phones to ask them to complete a series of particularly demanding tasks.[87] While driving, they had to listen to lists of words, then verbally solve maths problems, and between each maths problem, repeat back the next word in the list. It's a difficult test, made much more so by having to drive, follow another car, and speak on the phone at the same time. Tough.

Researchers had started by just looking for the limits of task-juggling, but results found that there was a group of exceptional individuals. These Super-Taskers could do all those tasks together just as well as they could do them separately. And they could perform those simultaneous tasks better than the best of the other participants could do any of them one at a time. Not all of them had realised just how unusual they were, but most effortlessly juggled many different tasks in their daily lives. And this is true of the many people who could develop their task-juggling skills or use those Nowist skills to keep more things moving forward, faster and better.

SOME BALLS ARE BIGGER THAN OTHERS

Not all tasks we juggle are equal; some are bigger, some are smaller, some are harder, and some are easier. Some individual tasks belong to different bigger tasks, and each task tends to belong to a particular sphere of work, goal or different stream of action.

So, it's one thing to juggle different tasks that belong to the same sphere or stream. You might move from chatting about a particular subject to doing something related to that same subject. Like talking about an exotic holiday with your family and then checking website reviews about that destination. Different tasks but same sphere.

You might be talking about what you've found out about the sunny beach or snow-covered mountain when a family member asks if you'd like to play a video game. Different task, different sphere, but same stream of action, because it's all about family and friends. Investing in relationships.

If your boss calls in the middle of your video game, and asks you to check out a website ahead of a meeting, then it's a different task, sphere and stream of action, it's all about work and career. It will often take more energy to switch, more energy to keep both tasks in mind, and more energy to return to the original task.

And your mood may have changed, even if you did remember what you were doing, and even if your family member is still waiting for you to continue.

People respond to such interruptions in different ways. Interruptions can be welcome if you're looking for a distraction from an unwanted task. They can be annoying if you have just started to concentrate and feel the energy drifting away. But they are less wasteful, and less irritating, when you accept and embrace interruptions as part of the natural flux of life.

In a study of hospital nurses it was found that interruptions and time pressure did not usually cause them to forget tasks, or be dissatisfied with their work, as long as they occurred during the first two-thirds of the working shift, when they were expected. It was only in the last part of the day, when people expected not to be interrupted, that those unplanned tasks became annoying.[88]

Nowists, much more than others, will tend to view interruptions as opportunities to do something different. There's the interruption itself, something new. There's the chance to deal smoothly with the unplanned, because to potentially fail is a test of Nowist adaptability. They embrace the new thoughts that are prompted by the interruption and whatever might happen as a result of the unexpected.

And because of their enthusiasm for the potential benefits of task-juggling, they actively look for ways to get better at jumping between spheres and streams of action. Thenists may avoid the kinds of activities that would make them better at fluidly and gracefully using the energy of life. They may refuse to try because they can't yet.

When your goals feel right you feel propelled forwards, and when they are fun you feel invigorated. When you feel that thrill, your energy is greater for many things, which means that it is generally better to do what fills you with energy than to drag yourself to do a single energy-draining task.

Effortful self-control, forcing yourself to focus on one task at the expense of another distracting task, is not as energy efficient as effortless self-motivation, being pulled forward by something that you love, or loving something you are doing. Finding the fun. Catching the buzz.

Of course, much of the work done in the world is

not joyful. Just as many outcomes and achievements, both ordinary and extraordinary, are the result of painful relentless effort, or simply neutral action. Yet this approach that uses energy while choosing to take pleasure in our actions is invigorating.

This is why those who love what they do, and love the flux and changes of life, are also those who also tend to live longest.[89] They move in harmony with naturally motivated streams of energy.

Moving between streams of activities is energising, and allows you to keep forward momentum even when there is a pause or a delay in other streams of action. Embracing more than one priority also makes it easier to act in harmony with your natural interest in more than one thing. You care about many things, you enjoy many things, you are made curious by many things, and you are good at many things, so why force yourself to settle for the over-focused, under-lived life?

MOVED BY THE MOMENT

Mind-wandering has been traditionally discouraged as a distraction, just as multi-tasking has been viewed as wasteful inefficiency, but what if for some people it's the other way around? What if the wandering mind can prevent the mind becoming stuck? And what if multi-tasking is better thought of as well suited to fluid intelligence in its natural element? Your brain rewarding you for the natural movement and problem-solving that allowed your predecessors to survive and evolve.

So when psychologists asked people to record their mind-wandering experiences, they found that interesting thoughts left them feeling happier, even when it took focus away from what they were doing.

And when, in another study, people were asked to complete a lengthy set of tests designed for their mind-numbing effects, people who let their minds wander off task often outperformed their on-task rivals.[90] This can be an important ability, the power to refresh your brain so you can see creative connections and opportunities for action. While Thenists are attempting to avoid mistakes at all costs, they may also miss the value hidden inside and outside the task.

As discussed in previous chapters, this ability to decouple attention from perception, to free yourself from the constraints of the situation, has significant benefits.

It allows you to better grasp and feel the overall meaning in a situation, particularly its meaning for you personally. You know what it means, and can preview different ways in which actions now will lead to good things both now and in the future. And it allows you to *follow* your feelings. It is not some knee-jerk impulsivity disconnected from what you value or seek. And nor is it some kind of fear-filled conformity that stops you moving towards an empowering delight in your ability to move, and to make better things happen.

This is what happens when you are moved by the moment, often with the feeling that you are in harmony with your extended self.

THE POWER OF FUN

When people were asked to do a difficult task well and motivate themselves, they completed the task well enough. But when they were asked to pretend that they found the difficult task enjoyable, they did better. They knew what fun felt like so they performed better until, after a while, it became too difficult to keep pretending that it was fun.

The valuable insight here is that fun makes difficult work easier but that it takes energy to *pretend* to have fun. Real self-motivation is easier to maintain because we anticipate what is required to keep working well, but the best of both worlds is the power to motivate action, or movement, that provides innate fun, joy and pleasure.

Fantasising about the future takes a lot of energy, and it takes that energy away from actively making things happen. The result can be a depressing gap between the positive fantasy and what ends up happening – which is almost always worse.

People in an experiment were asked to imagine their futures in a range of twelve different scenarios about achievement.[91] As a participant, you had to read each scenario description, such as being unable to meet a deadline for something really important and asking for an extension. Then you had to close your eyes and vividly imagine what would happen when you were called by the person who had the power to decide what would happen next . . .

Those who had constructed positive fantasies felt better in the very short term, in the time immediately after they had imagined good things just happening. But the surprising thing was that the people who wrote down the most positive fantasy endings to the scenarios were also the people who experienced the most depressive feelings over the next three months. The same thing happened for schoolchildren, students, and adults. It was an energy-draining approach to action in the present and future.

Nowists want to take effortless but challenging action, and will often choose to find fun in what they do or simply find fun things and do them.

They use their intelligence to learn from what they do, and so more accurately match present actions to what they have enjoyed doing in the past, and increase the likelihood of doing more of what they love in the future.

PART THREE
THE #NOWIST TOOLKIT

Toolkit 1:
NOWIST VS THENIST

You may have moved through this book in a blur or taken your time over every word. You may have leapt before you looked, and ended up here for a quick idea of what the book is about.

We're all at least a little bit Nowist. We can all enjoy movement, and taking action. But how Nowist or Thenist are you? And how well is it working for you? It is not just a fixed personality trait or ability. It is a flexible mindset that can be developed to provide forward motion.

We all live between the past and the future. We live in the present, and we can only directly think, do or change anything at the point of #Now.

This is a reminder of some of the differences between the two mindsets.

First: When you feel like a Thenist, tasks are a means to an end. You do things to look good or to get the task finished. You might forget to enjoy life. Nowists love moving, and seek joy in doing things. They don't want to waste their lives waiting for happiness, so they seek happiness now.

Second: Thenists are more likely to agonise about decisions. This can slow them down, they can procrastinate, or they can suddenly lurch into a decision that makes no sense. They can get stuck in a downwards spiral. Nowists make effortless, rapid or fast decisions. They see sequences, and they have a sense of where they are going.

Third: When in a Thenist mindset you can be easy to interrupt or slow down. Even distant worries can derail you, and leave you in a downwards spiral of inactivity and anticipated regret. You can work hard, but it feels like hard work, leaving you worn-out and overwhelmed. But when you're in a Nowist mindset, you can be hard to stop. You feel like a force of nature with almost limitless energy to keep moving forward. You see obstacles as opportunities, and stress as just another source of forward motion.

Fourth: Thenists tend to be self-doubting. They may second-guess their own judgement, even when they know they are factually right. Nowists tend to be self-trusting. They are confident in their abilities in general, and in particular their abilities to improve and learn. They develop a sense of personal power, not over others but to make good things happen. They test their ability and learn more about cause, effect. They also learn more about the meaning and value of their actions and outcomes.

Fifth: In a Thenist mindset, your energy can be wasted on worry, on going nowhere except self-defeating or passive directions. The worry steals from your positive present. In a Nowist mindset you have do-it energy. You invest time or energy in things you can change. And when you do start to worry, you quickly recognise the downwards spiral. You roll out of negativity and move forwards. You enjoy the power of #Now.

THENIST

1 Tasks as means
2 Slow decisions
3 Easy to interrupt
4 Self-doubting
5 What-if worry

past

#

future

NOWIST

1 Love moving
2 Fast decisions
3 Hard to stop
4 Self-trusting
5 Do-it energy

Toolkit 2:
MEET THE NOWISTS

In this book we've discussed several important differences between Nowists and Thenists, including how they manage their emotions, make decisions, respond to life stress and move forward. In this section we'll describe a few more different styles of different kinds of Nowist and Thenist mindsets that haven't been discussed.

Do you recognise yourself?

YOLO Thenists find many reasons for putting off the unpleasant work of making decisions, doing work or facing a future that is unwelcome or unsettling. In this mindset, 'You only live once' is more about not doing something than loving what you do. You are actively finding stuff to distract yourself because then you don't have to do whatever it is that you don't like. Sometimes this can be about laziness and not wanting to work – however, just as often you are very active but your actions are intended to avoid what you fear, rather than move you forward.

Fatalist Thenists conclude that there is nothing that can be done. They think, 'Oh, I'm going to mess this up,' or, 'Oh, this is just my luck. Over and over and over again.'* And from this perspective, simply to stop trying to make good things happen seems to make sense. You might stop doing everything, and sit, or curl up, passively. You might feel like doing nothing but continue to go through the motions of life and work. But you stop seeing the opportunities, or stop creating opportunities. Instead of finding out, you waste life hiding out.

Fantasist Thenists pretend that, as if by magic, everything is going to turn out wonderfully. They lose their forward momentum while dreaming of a perfect future. And they let the fantasy become so reassuring

---

* A couple of lines from the 2015 Imagine Dragons song 'Shots'. It was suggested by my son, Zak, who felt it summed up how he feels when in a negative Thenist spiral of self-doubt.

that they convince themselves that achieving it requires no effort on their part. You might even tell anyone who will listen about your vision or dream, and relish the pleasure of talking about the idea. This pleasure can become a substitute for the benefits of taking real-world steps towards making anything better, and then you are stunned and disappointed when the magic doesn't kick in.

Chicken-Licken Thenists are terrified that the absolute worst will happen. They fear that anything they do will lead to disaster, but also that whatever they *don't* decide to do will lead to something awful happening. It is a kind of dramatic, fright-night response to what *might* happen that ends up wasting valuable energy. When you feel like this, you might be active, even extremely active, but it is unlikely you will accomplish much of value since running around in a panic won't help anything. Better to take a calm look at what's really happening and figure out your next steps.

Passion Nowists are pulled towards what they love – or what they care most about changing. They have something that deeply moves them and they use that profound feeling to keep them moving forward. For instance, you might want to help the disadvantaged by campaigning for a better world. Or you build a business, or do a job, that creates what you think the world needs. It might be that you create opportunities to do what you love, or just help the people you love.

Action Nowists take great joy in moving fast and getting things done. While they may also care about the purpose of their work, for them the most important thing is the action, the speed and the thrill. They are all about saying 'Yes' to new challenges. They volunteer. They like to be busy and can be heard urging others to 'just get on with it'. They want quick payoffs as a reward for investing massive amounts of intense effort. Though many Action Nowists are extremely talented at planning meticulously – because it allows them to enjoy the thrill of amazing, death-defying actions – they sometimes could benefit from a little more looking ahead while leaping forward.

Power Nowists delight in moving as a means of confirming their sense of their own competence. They feel strong when they are *doing*, and doing makes them become even stronger: they get switched on by the exhilaration of being able to make things happen. Their force of will overcomes barriers and conventions and others move aside to make way for someone who is self-evidently a force of nature. They are motivated by their powerful ability to move mountains, make good things happen and motivate others to help and follow them.

Super-Nowists are those people who become extra-ordinarily good at everything that we've discussed in this book. They move forward at breath-taking speed. They have a stunningly clear idea of how things work, what they want and where they are going. They accomplish most, and love both the journey and the destination. Some of them are famous super-tasking, ground-breaking polymaths. Others bring an unusual calmness to demanding situations. They all demon-strate a remarkable capacity to grow to meet any stress or setback, and don't need the prospect of headlines or awards to motivate them. You may not be a Super-Nowist, or even want to be, but there's much to be learned from them about how to enjoy your #Now.

Toolkit 3:
NOWIST TEAMS AND CULTURE

The truth is that Nowists will tend to judge organisations not on structure but on whether that organisation gives them the opportunity to keep taking effortless action.

They'll prefer a fairly traditional hierarchy when it allows them to move quickly, or a no-rules, no-leaders environment when that works best for speed.

You'll find people joining the military – looking for thrills, to test themselves, to go faster. Or you'll find them gravitating to emergency medicine, or activism, or space exploration, or the newsroom. So, if you are an employer and want to attract Nowists and benefit from their ability to look while leaping, the best way is to ask yourself how well your company facilitates movement and pushing limits.

A firm like Valve Corporation, the creator of ground-breaking video games, believes in a different way of working. In principle, anyone can work on any project they want. And new projects can be created by anyone who can get other people to work on their project. They even have desks with wheels so that they can roll towards other people to form new teams. Spontaneous order in action – and all without the waste of fixed management structures and rules.

There's a lot to like in this kind of set-up for Nowists, but only when it doesn't stop their perpetual motion. With all that negotiating or convincing other people to go with you, you can sometimes feel as if you're not making any progress. So the trick is to tweak any organisational climate to make action and decisions more effortless, and less painful.

Equally, Nowists are better when they are able to see the negotiation process as part of the natural way of things, part of the change that they love. Then it stops being something to avoid, and starts being part of something they embrace. And when you work with other Nowists, you start to prioritise taking the next step forward rather than finding the perfect answer before you get started.

Another option to employ for making rapid progress

is to use what already exists – to plug into markets and systems that allow you to get moving without negotiation. The online markets, currently represented most famously by Alibaba, Amazon and eBay, all make it easier to make connections. You can get a prototype of your product design made anywhere in the world. You can get professional advice, or indeed almost any kind of service, from even the most far-flung locations on the planet.

Nowists want to find ways of moving faster, and are attracted to new ideas for increasing their speed. When they find these fresh concepts they want to quickly put them to work. This can be a huge advantage, but Nowists are often the trickiest to keep on your track, if your track isn't capable of speed or doesn't start soon enough.

You saying 'patience, patience', is not what they want to hear. They like to be busy, but they don't enjoy pretending to be busy. Instead they'll move towards what feels like real work, with a faster start and a more tangible sense of progress.

NOWISTS USE THEIR POWER TO EMPOWER

As a Nowist, it is good that you enjoy the advantages that come from being perceived as powerful. But being perceived as powerful can sometimes reduce the help you receive, and therefore limit your total power to make things happen. And that's not so good.

If your power makes others feel powerless, they'll be less likely to participate: why make suggestions if it looks as if you don't need them? They are less likely to correct you even when they know you are factually wrong. Fortunately, there are ways of moving fast and taking others with you.

First, if you're in Nowist mode, be aware of the power of your always-on, always-moving Nowness. It's hard to stop your flow. You make it pretty clear when you are bored, blocked or frustrated. You tend to move away from, or around, things that slow you down. And those 'things' include people. People who can feel trampled on, bulldozed or just unneeded.

Second, embrace the power of others – start seeing nurturing their power as something you want for yourself. When you want something as a Nowist, you tend to rapidly assess each situation for ways to get to your goal. As soon as you embrace empowering and collaborating with others, you will find it easier to naturally find joy in those activities.

Third, understand better how to make it clear that you are actively seeking the help of others. The evidence is clear: people want to know that you are open to their ideas, warnings and suggestions. They need to know that you are willing to be corrected, and what kind of help you need. And the faster you are moving, the more it is worthwhile figuring out how you can collaborate at speed.

EXPANDING YOUR NOW WITH THE NOW OF OTHERS

The best way of living and working with others is found when our Now is in harmony with the Now of others. When this happens, we experience a moment of meeting. Our priorities and shared rhythms slide into place smoothly and seamlessly.

Sometimes this can occur at a distance: people who are in harmony with you might not be aware of your existence but are still working towards very similar goals and ideals. You are in-sync, naturally moving with other people and what they produce and do.

This is what happens when two or more people are working to solve the same problem, or when they share the same priorities. More than ever before, it is possible to find someone else who is working on what you love too. And you can feel the power created when many people start to move together. #Now

Toolkit 4:
BREATHING DEEPLY, MOVING FORWARD

Do you ever feel stressed? Of course you do. And one way people will tell you how to cope is to lower your expectations, to avoid what might make you stronger. As you know, this book offers valuable insights into an alternative. You can choose instead to nurture a Nowist mindset. By seeking joy in the flow of life you will discover your natural power to take action and keep moving forward.

It's good to reach out for stress first-aid when you're feeling overwhelmed. But there are alternatives to relatively passive ways of dealing with the pressures of life and work. We tend to become overwhelmed when we don't clearly see a believable path to a better future. We feel trapped. We feel powerless. And we stop moving.

Once you start moving again, you will start to regain a feeling of power in your situation. You will begin to naturally reassert your ability to make good things happen. And it can often be enough to start by moving physically, even if that movement is not specific to what has caused or triggered your stress.

There is more than one way to feel present in the moment, or to open your mind to experiencing what is happening around you. Mindfulness has become an industry, supported by a certain amount of scientific research and many who say that it bring them benefits. All forms of mindfulness are based on older traditions of meditation, although the modern style is often practised without the spiritual and ritual elements.

There are other traditions, and modern equivalents, that are more physical and active. These more active forms of meditation, or any activity that helps clear thinking, may offer similar benefits along with the innate advantages and pleasure of movement.

THE ONE-MINUTE WORKOUT

Martin Gibala and his colleagues found that even one minute of intense exercise can be as effective as much longer exercise sessions.[92] Their surprising research showed people getting pretty much the same benefit from sixty-second bursts of intense movement as they did from longer, less intense exercise. About four minutes in total gave very similar physical gains to a traditional moderate level of intensity over forty-five minutes. It's good to remember that sometimes more intensity can make up for less time. Speed can stretch time.

GET UP, STAND UP

Another way of moving more is to just stand up rather than sitting down. There are standing-up desks that allow all the same access to paper and equipment, and these have been made available by some employers.[93] With mobile technology it is easy enough to keep working or entertaining yourself without staying in one place for long. You can stand and talk, stand and think, or take the next step by walking while you work. Other people use treadmills, or inside running tracks. The benefits to your body and your mind from getting your embodied self moving are self-evident.

YOGA, PILATES AND DANCING

Yoga reduces stress, and is linked with decreased blood pressure and heart rate.[94] It also reduces levels of cortisol, the steroid hormone that, if too high over time, can reduce the effectiveness of your immune system. Similar benefits have been proposed for dancing,[95] pilates[96] and tai chi, as well as Japan's regenerating movement exercise and Sufi whirling, originally practised in Iran and Turkey.

ONE-MINUTE MINDFULNESS

Many mindfulness books include one particular mental and physical exercise. You breathe deeply, often with your eyes closed, and then watch your feelings floating above you, temporarily separate from you. You can see your feelings as responses to things rather than as things themselves.[97] Our responses can change, even when particular facts cannot. As you breathe, and let your feelings float like clouds above you, you can start to feel more in control, less overwhelmed. That change in perspective protects you and lets you start moving again.[98]

The above does not represent a recommendation of any particular activity. The levels of research vary, and the effectiveness will depend on you and your preferences. It is a reminder that there are many available activities that get you rolling, can get you clear-headed, and help you move forward.

Toolkit 5:
SENSE OF NOWNESS

Your sense of nowness is the product of your brain networks interacting with each other and with the external world. There are many networks and many neural patterns that connect them in almost innumerable ways, based on genetics, our inherited nature and our experiences.

Of these, two are the most relevant to our purposes. There is the action-oriented Now network, which spirals forward from decision to action. And the more speculative, state-oriented Then network, which is always switched on – cycling through thoughts of the self, the past, present and future.

When this is working effectively, your Then network

unconsciously processes what has happened, speculates about yourself, and plays with many possibilities; your brain works away, always thinking, even when you sleep. Your goals can change, and you can process information that can help you move towards your goals without you even knowing that it has happened.

As a result, your Then network often does its best work in the background, and will be turned down when it is time to make a decision or take action.

You want the available energy available for choosing or doing. This includes consciously thinking about specific alternatives but it is different from the less conscious, less controlled thoughts of your Then. It is thinking that is directed by your Now. It is your Now that takes action, and consciously considers action, while flexibly communicating with your emotions, memories, verbatim facts and gist meanings.

To better understand the way they work together, neuroscientists have used various techniques, including brain imaging. As a human, one of the big individuals differences in the ability to look while leaping, and leap while looking, is the connectivity between parts of your brain. It is not just about the parts – many animals share those – or the relative size of those parts. It is about the many connections and networks that allow those parts to be accessed and used in more powerful ways.

The Nowist mindset is marked out by greater neural flexibility, openness and connectivity. And although the brain science will continue to evolve, the overall benefits of flexibility and connectivity will remain. You can use this to help yourself recognise when your Then network is overheating because of prolonged feelings of stress and worry that do not lead to active, purposeful movement forward.

You can exert some level of flexible control over your use of mental energy, and you're doing it right now. You're diverting some of your mental energy into these words, then perhaps questioning the arguments and testing them against your own experiences. Nowists become effective at moving between Then and Now.

Toolkit 6:
NOWIST IDEAS AND SCIENCE

The Nowist mindset described in this book is supported by a combination of scientific theory and research findings.

While there is no one-to-one correlation between these underpinnings and Nowists, Thenists and the concepts of Nowness and #Now, there *are* many different sources that help to explain and reveal aspects of how these all fit together. Here are a few of the thinkers who have provided powerful and surprising cutting-edge insights.

Arie W. Kruglanski & E. Tory Higgins
University of Maryland & Columbia University

There's a whole international community of researchers working on regulatory mode theory (RMT), which proposes ways that locomotion and assessment both independently influence our behaviour. Yet it is not science that is well known outside of academic psychological journals. Hopefully this book will help to change that. Kruglanski and Higgins, both famous for other research, came up with the theory after an afternoon's skiing when they realised how differently they approached everything, including snow, mountains and sunscreen. RMT is all about the difference between 'doing the right thing' and 'just doing it', the joy of doing and the agony of indecision.

Scott J. Dickman
University of Massachusetts-Dartmouth

It seems fairly likely that Dickman's work would be much better known if he had not died tragically early. He was only able to make a small start on researching the important difference between dysfunctional impulsivity, the kind that gets you into trouble, and functional impulsivity, the kind that lets you choose quickly and calmly. It is a behavioural trait that explains some of the Nowist's preference for effortless decisions, and something only discovered by looking carefully at some unexpected results from a clever experiment into perception conducted at the University of Texas.

Julius Kuhl
Max Planck Institute for Psychological Research
The big idea from Kuhl is Personality System Interactions Theory. He described different systems that interact to shape how you respond in particular situations. Purpose memory gives a sense of reason, while extension memory gives a sense of self. When relaxed, you are able to take actions in harmony with this sense of self. And because Nowists tend to stay relaxed, even under pressure, they are more likely to act in harmony with their sense of self. Of particular interest to an understanding of a Nowist is Kuhl's theory of self-regulation. He makes a distinction between two orientations: action-orientation, the tendency to take action and the ability to regulate those actions effectively; and state-orientation, the tendency to be concerned about the gap between the state you're in and possible states in the past, present or future. These are not the same as Kruglanski's concepts but they are helpful. Nowists are high locomotors, but also highly action-oriented. They can look while leaping.

Charles J. Brainerd & Valerie F. Reyna
Cornell University

Sometimes you can remember facts without being able to use them effectively to figure something out. Or you can figure something out based on very few facts, or without consciously recalling those facts. These differences led Brainerd and Reyna to propose what's called Fuzzy Trace Theory, which describes verbatim memory for facts and gist memory for meaning or patterns. You have both but each person will differ in how well each is developed. This means some people, including Nowists, can use their gist memory ability to intuitively understand deep underlying patterns. This reasoning is rapid and may seem to come effortlessly but it is not lazy or dysfunctional.

Marcus E. Raichle
Washington University School of Medicine

First he made the discoveries that allowed scans of brain functioning via strong magnetic waves, known as magnetic resonance imaging or MRI. Then he used this Functional MRI to accidentally discover something called the Default Mode Network: that your brain has a default mode that is always on, and that the parts of your brain involved with the default mode network usually turn themselves down when taking action or making choices. Since then the DMN has been joined by other neural networks that give us a better idea of how brain connectivity and flexibility are what makes us human. Raichle believes that this background ability, to imagine possibilities and compare them to what our future self wants, is important for creativity, survival and action.

Endnote:
LET'S START (AGAIN) WITH #NOW

L ife. It all happens at the same time. #Now.

Your life is what still happens when you're busy trying to become unbusy. Life is the thing that happens all at once while you try to find that one thing to focus upon. Life is priorities, plural – not priority, singular. Nowists tend to dive into streams of the unplanned and planned. Rather than feeling time-poor, they feel experience-rich. The surprise, the shock, the event, the never-again and the ordinary or extraordinary.

One danger of viewing busy as an automatically bad thing is that people can waste their time trying to avoid the unavoidable. A second is that people can become unhappy looking for the unfindable – that one perfect priority. And a third pitfall is that we may incorrectly view work and activity as bad-busyness rather than as good-busyness! This is life, and having a full life can be wonderful.

Busy is just one way of describing action. The Nowist approach is to tip towards motion that is positive and forward-directed. So we can love fixing that roof, paying those bills, attending that meeting, and feel satisfaction in what we choose to do – even when what we choose might in other circumstances be seen as an obligation. Having to do a thing can often become loving to do that same thing.

Every situation is unique, naturally, yet there is a danger of viewing busy as automatically abnormal and unhealthy. We like to feel effective. We can like to be active. We are often better off embracing action rather than resenting being made to move or change. The only way to stop is to die. Movement is life. And, as my grandfather would say, life is generally the better of the two alternatives.

Notes

Introduction

1 The importance of making the most of the moment – particularly given that we will not live for ever – continues to inspire poetic statements, aphorisms, sayings and song lyrics. Most recently, the Canadian rapper Drake helped popularise the motto YOLO, an acronym for 'You Only Live Once', but 165 years before that Johann Strauss published a waltz with exactly the same title in German, 'Man Lebt Nur Einmal!' There's also FOMO, the Fear Of Missing Out, and the classic Latin phrase *Carpe Diem* ('seize the day'), which was coined by the Roman poet Horace nearly 2,000 years ago. Horace's meaning was that it is better to take action today because tomorrow is uncertain.

Chapter 1: Always Moving Forward (The Need for Speed)

2 Dickman, S. J. (1985), 'Impulsivity and perception: individual differences in the processing of the local and global dimensions of stimuli', *Journal of Personality and Social Psychology*, 48(1), p. 133.

3 Dickman, S. J. (1990), 'Functional and dysfunctional impulsivity: personality and cognitive correlates', *Journal of Personality and Social Psychology*, 58(1), p. 95.

4 Higgins, E. T., & Kruglanski, A. W. (1995), 'A theory of regulatory modes: When locomotion versus assessment is emphasized', unpublished manuscript, Columbia University, New York.

Kruglanski told me that the origins of the idea came when he and long-term collaborator Tory Higgins both found themselves in a freezing blizzard at the top of a ski slope. Arie explained, 'I took one look at the weather conditions and launched myself down the mountain like a bat out of hell.' Tory, despite the bitter cold, continued to stretch his body, adjust his gloves, skies, boots, and googles, while assessing the best route down the slope. After getting back to the warmth of a bar, they discussed what guided the individual differences in their behaviours. This insight led to regulatory mode theory, the overarching theory into which assessment and locomotion mode fit.

5 Kruglanski, A. W., Thompson, E. P., Higgins, E. T., Atash, M., Pierro, A., Shah, J. Y., & Spiegel, S. (2000), 'To "do the right thing" or to "just do it": locomotion and assessment as distinct self-regulatory imperatives', *Journal of Personality and Social Psychology*, 79(5), p. 793.

6 Or, to give the award its full name, the Nobel Memorial Prize in Economic Sciences,

which Daniel Kahneman shared in 2002 with Vernon L. Smith. His decades of empirical work questioned whether the traditional assumptions made by economists about human rationality were accurate. In a series of clever experiments, often devised with his partner-in-trouble-making, Amos Tversky, who died in 1996 and so did not receive an award, Kahneman demonstrated a series of differences between assumed and actual human reasoning. Some of these discoveries about departures from economic rationality were less surprising to psychologists, who were quite used to human reasoning in the wild. Other discoveries were criticised by some for being little more than magic tricks. Yes, they cleverly demonstrated blind spots or biases, but these did not add up to irrationality. At least not in the real environments where people lived and worked. Our systems for reasoning have served us well, critics like Gigerenzer said, and should be judged according to their ecological rationality – by how often they lead to good outcomes given the nature of human preferences and our need to live and decide in the real world, in real time.

If you've been to a bookshop recently but don't read a lot of academic journals, you might know Kahneman better from his million-copy best-selling book, *Thinking, Fast and Slow*, in which he sets out a fairly long list of what he calls biases – and what others might call features – of human reasoning. He argues that the biases lead to systematic errors, and that both arise when we lazily allow our fast, go-with-your-gut system for thinking – our system 1 – to do the figuring out rather than put our system 2 – our slow, deliberative system for thinking – to work. Even when we could have calculated something accurately, particularly how likely something is, with a bit more effort, we go with the less effortful option. Some of us are prepared, like Dickman's functional impulsives or Kruglanski's locomotors, to go with less accuracy, for less effort, or less effort for faster results, but Nowists just as often get equally accurate results with less obvious effort.

7 Jaffe, E. (2004), 'What Was I Thinking? Kahneman Explains How Intuition Leads Us Astray', *APS Observer*, 17(5), pp. 24–26. In this article Eric Jaffe reports on the March 2004 Kahneman lecture at the National Institutes of Health where he explained

several computational flaws in decisions made by people in his experiments, and also points out that while 'most of our mental life is relatively effortless', we should try to 'recognise situations in which our intuition is likely to lead us astray'.

It is a point he comes back to in the 2009 article written for respected journal *American Psychologist* with Gary Klein, advocate for decisions in the real world, or naturalistic decision-making, in which they both set out conditions for intuitive expertise, and announced their failure to disagree.

Kahneman, D., & Klein, G. (2009), 'Conditions for Intuitive Expertise: A Failure to Disagree', *American Psychologist*, 64(6), p. 515.

8 In his delightful book *In Praise of Slow* Carl Honoré refers to *tempo giusto*, a musical term 'whose mission is to persuade conductors, orchestras, and soloists' to find the best speed, rather than assume that playing as fast as possible is always best. He also mentions a German movement with its own word, *eigenzeit*, own speed, which suggests that 'every living being has its own inherent time or pace'. This idea of having one's own speed is intuitively appealing.

Chapter 2: Keep Your #Now Moving

9 Furtner, M. R., Rauthmann, J. F., & Sachse, P. (2013), 'Unique self-leadership: A bifactor model approach', *Leadership*, 1742715013511484. http://lea.sagepub.com/content/early/2013/11/18/17427150135114 84.abstract

Lucke, G. A., & Furtner, M. R. (2015), 'Soldiers lead themselves to more success: A self-leadership intervention study'. *Military Psychology*, 27(5), p. 311. http://psycnet.apa.org/journals/mil/27/5/311/

Panagopoulos, N. G., & Ogilvie, J. (2015), 'Can salespeople lead themselves? Thought self-leadership strategies and their influence on sales performance', *Industrial Marketing Management*, 47, pp. 190–203. http://www.sciencedirect.com/science/article/pii/S0019850115000784

10 This has great similarities to a concept proposed by James Gibson, over at Cornell University, who was one of the greatest psychologists of the twentieth century. He used the term 'affordances' to describe opportunities for action in the environment. It was later suggested, by William Gaver, that

they could be categorised into perceived affordances, the opportunities for action that you notice, hidden affordances, which are there but not noticed, and false affordances, which offer opportunities for action that turn out to be misleading.

11 Avnet, T., & Higgins, E. T. (2003), 'Locomotion, assessment, and regulatory fit: Value transfer from "how" to "what"', *Journal of Experimental Social Psychology*, 39(5), pp. 525–530.

12 This is known as psychological well-being, and there are six dimensions, relating to autonomy, mastery, purpose, growth, relationships and self-acceptance. The first three may be familiar if you've read Steve Pink's book *Drive*, which explains their importance in motivation based on Deci and Ryan's Self-Determination Theory. Psychological well-being was developed by Carol Ryff and published back in 1989. She contrasts it with another measure of happiness, known as subjective well-being, which examines how people experience their lives, and whether they experience more positive or negative emotions overall.

Ryff, C. D. (1989), 'Happiness is everything, or is it? Explorations on the meaning of psychological well-being', *Journal of Personality and Social Psychology*, 57(6), p. 1,069.

13 Kupor, D. M., Tormala, Z. L., & Norton, M. I. (2014), 'The allure of unknown outcomes: Exploring the role of uncertainty in the preference for potential', *Journal of Experimental Social Psychology*, 55, pp. 210–216. Also, Tormala, Z. L. (2016), 'The role of certainty (and uncertainty) in attitudes and persuasion', *Current Opinion in Psychology*, 10, pp. 6–11, where it is argued that uncertainty can be 'strategically added' to influence uncertainty-oriented potential-lovers. More valuable in this book is the idea that Nowists can influence themselves by focusing on potential, which is more interesting, rather than track record, thus inspiring them to keep moving forward.

14 John Atkinson, a psychologist who worked out of the University of Michigan for his whole thirty-five-year career, explored how some people do not move towards more difficult, more rewarding challenges even after they have successfully completed less difficult, less challenging tasks. The question

led to the theory of achievement motivation, where some people want to succeed, and others try to avoid failure. Nowists are success-oriented because they want the joyful reward that comes from finding success *after* seeking success. They love the chase and the challenge.

Some psychologists argue that success-oriented people would choose medium-difficulty tasks because they would allow them to *feel* a sense of accomplishment in successfully completing the task. Too hard, and they might not succeed – which they want. Too easy, and they might not feel successful – which they also want.

Later work by Richard Sorrentino and colleagues also looked at what motivates one person to choose a difficult task, another an easy task, and others to opt for medium-difficulty tasks. They argued that it isn't just feeling good or bad that drives people to make their choice, but instead they were motivated by pathways that helped them to gain new self-knowledge or helped them to maintain their existing self-knowledge.

Sorrentino, R. M. (2012), 'Uncertainty orientation: A theory where the exception forms the rule', *REME*, 1576, p. 4,214.

15 Now with assets of more than $17 billion, Musk recently welcomed 365,000 – yep, three-hundred-and-sixty-five-thousand – pre-orders for his latest electric vehicle. The Tesla Model 3 will be the lowest-priced Tesla vehicle, with a cost of about $35,000. He also enjoyed witnessing a successful landing of his reusable rocket onto a floating platform, and signing a deal with NASA to send its astronauts into space. The plan for making Mars inhabitable hasn't happened yet, and that's the whole attraction. It provides a whole lot of uncertain space – Mars is about 250 million miles away with about 55 million square miles of land to terraform – into which Musk can move forward.

16 Amato, C., Pierro, A., Chirumbolo, A., & Pica, G. (2014), 'Regulatory modes and time management: How locomotors and assessors plan and perceive time', *International Journal of Psychology*, 49(3), pp. 192–199.

17 People in a more Thenist mindset tend to focus on how other people may criticise them. They also think a lot about all the ways their future selves may criticise what they have done. They think about the future in

such a scattergun way that they experience generalised pain regarding imagined regrets, and humiliation relating to actions not yet taken. And it's all pain, no gain, because their mental time travel is too vague to provide any specific guidance. Even when they think about good things in the future, it tends to be at a fantasy level. They may be a temporary escape, or a habitual distraction, but they don't really contribute much to moving forward.

Dysfunctionally impulsive people may also do things quickly but they do so in a disconnected way. If you also tend to worry about the difference between where you are – the present state – and where you might end up – the future state – then you suffer twice. Your future and present are disconnected, and you are worried about the existence of the gap rather than pragmatically moving forward to build bridges, ride the rapids, cross ravines, or climb mountains. You are stuck, or you are lost, unless you let your inner Nowist move you forward.

18 Pierro, A., Giacomantonio, M., Pica, G., Kruglanski, A. W., & Higgins, E. T. (2013), 'Locomotion and the preference for multi-tasking: Implications for well-being', *Motivation and Emotion*, 37(2), pp. 213–223.

19 Coviello, D., Ichino, A., & Persico, N. (2014), 'Time allocation and task juggling', *The American Economic Review*, 104(2), pp. 609–623.

20 O'Connor, P. J., & Jackson, C. (2008), 'Learning to be saints or sinners: The indirect pathway from sensation seeking to behavior through mastery orientation', *Journal of Personality*, 76(4), pp. 733–752 and Jackson, C. J. (2011), 'How sensation seeking provides a common basis for functional and dysfunctional outcomes', *Journal of Research in Personality*, 45(1), pp. 29–36.

21 Smillie, L. D., & Jackson, C. J. (2006), 'Functional impulsivity and reinforcement sensitivity theory', *Journal of Personality*, 74(1), pp. 47–84.

22 Heyes, S. B., Adam, R. J., Urner, M., van der Leer, L., Bahrami, B., Bays, P. M., & Husain, M. (2012), 'Impulsivity and rapid decision-making for reward', *Frontiers in Psychology*, 3, p. 153.

23 Rutt, J. L., & Löckenhoff, C. E. (2016), 'From past to future: Temporal self-continuity across the life span', *Psychology and Aging*; Blouin-Hudon, E. M. C., & Pychyl, T. A. (2015), 'Experiencing the temporally extended self: Initial support for the role of affective states, vivid mental imagery, and future self-continuity in the prediction of academic procrastination', *Personality and Individual Differences*, 86, pp. 50–5; Adelman, R. M., Herrmann, S. D., Bodford, J. E., Barbour, J. E., Graudejus, O., Okun, M. A., & Kwan, V. S. (2016), 'Feeling closer to the future self and doing better: Temporal psychological mechanisms underlying academic performance', *Journal of Personality*; Macrae, C. N., Mitchell, J. P., Tait, K. A., McNamara, D. L., Golubickis, M., Topalidis, P. P., & Christian, B. M. (2015), 'Turning I into me: Imagining your future self', *Consciousness and Cognition*, 37, pp. 207–213; Oyserman, D., Destin, M., & Novin, S. (2015), 'The context-sensitive future self: Possible selves motivate in context, not otherwise', *Self and Identity*, 14(2), pp. 173–188.

24 Tu, Y., & Soman, D. (2014), 'The categorization of time and its impact on task initiation', *Journal of Consumer Research*, 41(3), pp. 810–822.

25 Rosenbaum, D. A., Gong, L., & Potts, C. A. (2014), 'Pre-crastination hastening subgoal completion at the expense of extra physical effort', *Psychological Science*, 0956797614532657; Richter, M. (2015), 'Commentary: Pre-crastination: hastening subgoal completion at the expense of extra physical effort', *Frontiers in Psychology*, p. 6.

Wasserman, E. A., & Brzykcy, S. J. (2015), 'Pre-crastination in the pigeon', *Psychonomic Bulletin & Review*, 22(4), pp. 1,130–1,134.

26 Arbulu, A., Usabiaga, O., & Castellano, J. (2015), 'A time motion analysis of lead climbing in the 2012 men's and women's world championship finals', *International Journal of Performance Analysis in Sport*, 15(3), pp. 924–934.

27 Pica, G., Amato, C., Pierro, A., & Kruglanski, A. W. (2015), 'The early bird gets the worm: On locomotors' preference for morningness', *Personality and Individual Differences*, 76, pp. 158–160.

28 Robert Vallerand is a Canadian psychologist who worked on some of the most influential motivational research of the past forty years alongside Ryan and Deci, which has since been made more famous by Dan Pink's bestseller *Drive*. His recent work has been the dualistic theory of passion, which sets out differences between obsessive passion and harmonious passion. There is evidence that suggests that some people are rarely passionate, but that those who are may experience different levels and flavours of passion. You can read more about his work here: Vallerand, R. J. (2016), 'The dualistic model of passion: Theory, research, and implications for the field of education', in Liu, Woon Chia, Wang, John Chee Keng & **Ryan**, Richard M. (eds), *Building Autonomous Learners*, pp. 31–58. Springer Singapore; Vallerand, R. J., Salvy, S. J., Mageau, G. A., Elliot, A. J., Denis, P. L., Grouzet, F. M., & Blanchard, C. (2007), 'On the role of passion in performance', *Journal of Personality*, 75(3), pp. 505–534; Vallerand, R. J., Blanchard, C., Mageau, G. A., Koestner, R., Ratelle, C., Léonard, M., & Marsolais, J. (2003), '*Les passions de l'ame*: on obsessive and harmonious passion', *Journal of Personality and Social Psychology*, 85(4), p. 756; Moeller, J., Keiner, M., & Grassinger, R. (2015), 'Two sides of the same coin: Do the dual types of passion describe distinct subgroups of individuals?' Journal of Person-Oriented Research, 1(3), pp. 131–150.

29 Bélanger, J. J., Pierro, A., Kruglanski, A. W., Vallerand, R. J., De Carlo, N., & Falco, A. (2015), 'On feeling good at work: The role of regulatory mode and passion in psychological adjustment', *Journal of Applied Social Psychology*, 45(6), pp. 319-329.

30 Van Putten, Marijke, Marcel Zeelenberg, Eric van Dijk, and Orit E. Tykocinski, 'Inaction inertia', *European Review of Social Psychology* 24, no. 1 (2013): pp. 123–159; van Putten, M., Zeelenberg, M., & van Dijk, E. (2010), 'Who throws good money after bad? Action vs. state orientation moderates the sunk cost fallacy', *Judgment and Decision Making*, 5(1), p. 33 and Zeelenberg, M., Nijstad, B. A., van Putten, M., & Van Dijk, E. (2006), 'Inaction inertia, regret, and valuation: A closer look', *Organizational Behavior and Human Decision Processes*, 101(1), pp. 89–104.

Chapter 3: Because Effortless Is Not Lazy

31 Evans, A. (2016), *Fuzzy-Trace Theory And The Neural Basis Of The Framing Effect In Adolescents*, Cornell Theses and Dissertations.

32 Fuzzy-trace Theory is a model of thinking and memory originally proposed by Valerie Reyna and the improbably named Charles Brainerd, both neuroscientists working at Cornell University's Human Neuroscience Institute. They presented it as a new intuitionism back in the 1990s to explain empirical findings that could not be explained by dual process models.

33 Brainerd, C. J., & Reyna, V. F. (1990), 'Gist is the grist: Fuzzy-trace theory and the new intuitionism', *Developmental Review*, 10(1), pp. 3–47.

34 Parasuraman, R., & Jiang, Y. (2012), 'Individual differences in cognition, effect, and performance: Behavioral, neuroimaging, and molecular genetic approaches', *Neuroimage*, 59(1), pp. 70–82.

35 This is from an article by Kevin Mitchell in the *Guardian*, 21 May 2016, which discusses Mauresmo no longer working with Murray. She says, 'Andy is complex. On the court, he can be the opposite of what he is off court. It can be confusing.' In many ways, Murray's success is all the more impressive because he appears to have to talk himself out of emotional overload and then talk himself back into the zone. Source : https://www.theguardian.com/sport/2016/may/21/andy-murray-amelie-mauresmo-on-court-behaviour-split

36 Andy revealed this in an interview in the *Mail on Sunday* in February 2015, following his fourth defeat to Novak Djokovic, which occurred despite his opponent appearing to be 'on the brink of a physical breakdown'. He also shared how his work with psychologists and psychiatrists has taught him 'a little bit about how the mind works' – that in some ways emotional outbursts are natural but that he knows that screaming at himself, and yelling up at his team, was 'self-defeating'.

37 Parasuraman and his colleagues found good performers had reduced activity in the posterior precuneus. It's the bit of you that is found towards the back middle (posteromedial) on the outer layer, or cortex,

of your brain. Recent findings, as discussed elsewhere in this book, consider it part of the default-mode network. The default-mode network appears to play an important 'always-on, always-scheming' role, which is useful until it overpowers all useful action, or simply gets in the way of joy in effortless movement towards desirable outcomes.

38 Sartre, J. P. (1987), *Huis clos,* Psychology Press.

39 This is how the AFP reported Spieth's Attack of the Thenist, 'Walking onto the 10th tee, Jordan Spieth looked cucumber cool and seemingly totally in charge of the Masters, five shots clear of the field. Two holes and some 20 minutes later – down in the depths of Amen Corner – he was a wreck, telling his caddie Mike Greller: "Buddy, it seems like we are collapsing."'

40 Nowists worry much less about what might have been, or what might have happened if they had simply done nothing. And they are more likely to regret not taking action. The complete opposite tends to happen with Thenists, who are distressed and distracted by the consequences of their actions. When you start to think like this, you are less and less likely to take action. This is costly because, all things being equal, only your own actions can really be trusted to improve your own situation. Nowists have that advantage.

41 The average times for the 40-yard dash in the NFL Scouting Combine, a week-long event where college players try to impress professional scouts, ranged from 4.55 seconds for wide receivers to 5.36 seconds for offensive guards. Bo Jackson, an all-star in baseball and football, weighed 210 pounds and claims to have run the 40 yards (in which times benefit from a running start) in 4.13 seconds. The average weight of the heaviest NFL players is over 300 pounds, according to official data for the 2013 season as compiled by Tomer Cohen, blogger.

42 'The Rule of 26–27–60 helps predict NFL quarterback success or failure', CNN, 8 July 2010.

43 Welter, J. C. (2013), 'The Wonderlic Classic Cognitive Ability Test as a measure of player selection and success for Quarterbacks in the National Football League' (Doctoral dissertation, Capella University).

44 Hickmann, S. A. (2004). 'Impulsivity as a Predictor of Athletic success and Negative Consequences in NFL football players' (Doctoral Dissertations Available from Proquest). Paper AAI3136735. http:// scholarworks.umass.edu/dissertations/ AAI3136735

45 Known as *Flanker Tests*, these involve giving participants a line of letters. The letter in the middle of the line is flanked by letters to either side. Those letters are either the same, known as congruent, or different, known as incongruent strings. In this particular experiment, participants were given a variation of the flanker test, with three-by-three letter grids, with the middle letter either congruent or incongruent. The idea is that congruent grids are recognised faster. That's also what happened in this experiment.

46 De Lange, M.A., & Van Knippenberg, A., 'To err is human: How regulatory focus and action orientation predict performance following errors', *Journal of Experimental Social Psychology*, Elsevier, 2009, 45 (6), p. 1,192.

47 This interest in winning or losing is referred to in different ways by psychologists. Sometimes it is described as the difference between promotion, wanting to make something good happen, and prevention, wanting to prevent something bad happening. And sometimes it is described along the lines of avoidance, wanting to avoid something bad, and approach-orientation, wanting to gain something good. If you put it together, you'll find some people (passively) avoiding bad things, while others try actively to ensure nothing bad happens. Nowists are naturally active seekers of good things – they want to make good things happen now!

48 In a series of experiments, Barbie Huelser and Janet Metcalfe, both psychologists at Columbia University, showed that making mistakes in one set of tests improved memory for the correct answer during subsequent tests. Participants remembered that two words were a pair, if they were shown that they had previously thought, mistakenly, that the two words were not a pair. This advantage seems to come from an overall gist memory, because the people doing the tests did not realise that past errors were helping them to remember.

Huelser, B. J., & Metcalfe, J. (2012), 'Making related errors facilitates learning, but learners do not know it', *Memory & Cognition*, 40(4), pp. 514–527.

49 Nowists prefer to decide quickly for four main reasons. First, because they love moving forward, and tip naturally to anything that allows them to move fluidly to action. Second, because they see advantages in grabbing opportunities now that can lead to better things later. Third, because they know that doing a lot of something is likely to lead to more wins than losses. And fourth because they have become, through talent and practice, better than the people around them at turning quick decisions into actions that lead to better outcomes. Telling a Nowist to slow down is often just a waste of their ability to use the #Now.

50 Connolly, T. (1999), 'Action as a fast and frugal heuristic', *Minds and Machines*, 9(4), pp. 479–496.

51 Klein, G., & Wright, C. (2016), 'Macrocognition: From theory to toolbox', *Frontiers in Psychology*, 7, p. 54.

52 https://www.theguardian.com/football/2012/may/17/wayne-rooney-visualisation-preparation

53 'Is Steph Curry the best shooter ever? Yes, say many of NBA's all-time marksmen', Bleacherreport.com. 1 June 2015. Retrieved 1 June 2015.

54 Vladimir Malakhov said blitz chess, or speed chess, was a 'waste of time', Bobby Fischer complained that it 'kills your ideas', while Nigel Short dramatically claimed that it 'rots the brain'.

55 According to Pal Benton, grandmaster and student of the game, for 'great attacking players as Bronstein and Tal, most combinations are inspired by the player's memories of earlier games.'

56 The longest-ever chess game was played for over twenty hours between Ivan Nikolic and Goran Arsovic in 1989. The match ended in a draw after 269 moves.

57 Tal, M., & Neat, K. P. (1976, 1997), 'The life and games of Mikhail Tal', *Everyman Chess* (2nd revised edition).

58 Fernand Gobet, a cognitive psychologist who has studied chess cognition for twenty-five years, part of the Swiss national chess team and a chess master, makes the point people can be high or low, good or bad, at fast-intuition, or pattern matching, and slow-deliberation, or searching. He suggests Tal was high on both. As are our Nowists, both as a way of living and a way of getting things done. This is explained in much more detail in his paper, Gobet, F. (2012), 'Concepts without intuition lose the game: Commentary on Montero and Evans (2011)', *Phenomenology and the Cognitive Sciences*, 11(2), pp. 237–250 and also in his 2015 book, Gobet, F. (2015), *Understanding Expertise: A Multi-disciplinary Approach* (Palgrave Macmillan).

59 Moxley, J. H., Ericsson, K. A., Charness, N., & Krampe, R. T. (2012), 'The role of intuition and deliberative thinking in experts' superior tactical decision-making', *Cognition*, 124(1), pp. 72–78.

Chapter 4: The Surprising Power Of Now: There's Only One Way to Find Out

60 Hepler, J., Albarracin, D., McCulloch, K. C., & Noguchi, K. (2012), 'Being active and impulsive: The role of goals for action and inaction in self-control', *Motivation and Emotion*, 36(4), pp. 416–424.

61 One remarkably helpful acronym for such times is HALT. Are you hungry? Angry? Lonely? Or tired? Developed by therapists working with people suffering from downward spirals of emotions, to quickly self-diagnose and self-nurture when you are feeling stressed-out tired, and passively-deflated.

62 Thayer, R. E. (2012), 'Moods of energy and tension that motivate', in Ryan, Richard M. (ed.), *The Oxford Handbook of Human Motivation*, p. 408.

63 http://www.dailymail.co.uk/sport/othersports/article-2926113/Tom-Daley-aiming-high-new-twister-dive-repertoire-pursuit-titles.html

64 Kruglanski, A. W., Pierro, A., Higgins, E. T., & Capozza, D. (2007), '"On the Move" or "Staying Put": Locomotion, Need for Closure, and Reactions to Organizational Change' *Journal of Applied Social Psychology*, 37(6), pp. 1,305–1,340.

65 Kumashiro, M., Rusbult, C. E., Finkenauer, C., & Stocker, S. L. (2007), 'To think or to do: The impact of assessment and locomotion orientation on the Michelangelo phenomenon', *Journal of Social and Personal Relationships*, 24(4), pp. 591–611.

66 Galinsky, A. D., Gruenfeld, D. H., & Magee, J. C. (2003). 'From power to action', *Journal of Personality and Social Psychology*, 85(3), p. 453 and Huang, L., Galinsky, A. D., Gruenfeld, D. H., & Guillory, L. E. (2010), 'Powerful postures versus powerful roles, which is the proximate correlate of thought and behavior?', *Psychological Science*.

67 https://candiesandcrunches. com/2014/02/21/ push-ups-101-a-cheaters-guide-to-lousy-push-ups-35-push-up-variations-and-fast-effective-bodyweight-upper-body-workout/

Chapter 5: Your Happy Now: Finding Joy In Your #Now

68 Baldwin, M. W., Carrell, S. E., & Lopez, D. F. (1990), 'Priming relationship schemas: My advisor and the Pope are watching me from the back of my mind', *Journal of Experimental Social Psychology*, 26(5), pp. 435–454.

69 Mullet, D. R., & Rinn, A. N. (2015), 'Giftedness and ADHD: Identification, misdiagnosis, and dual diagnosis', *Roeper Review*, 37(4), pp. 195–207.

70 Bonanno, G. A. (2004), 'Loss, trauma, and human resilience: Have we underestimated the human capacity to thrive after extremely aversive events?' *American Psychologist*, 59(1), p. 20; Galatzer-Levy, I. R., & Bonanno, G. A. (2016), 'It's not so easy to make resilience go away: Commentary on Infurna and Luthar', *Perspectives on Psychological Science*, 11(2), pp. 195–198; Hobfoll, S. E., Stevens, N. R., & Zalta, A. K. (2015), 'Expanding the science of resilience: conserving resources in the aid of adaptation', *Psychological Inquiry*, 26(2), pp. 174–180; Mancini, A. D., Bonanno, G. A., & Sinan, B. (2015), 'A brief retrospective method for identifying longitudinal trajectories of adjustment following acute stress', *Assessment*, 22(3), pp. 298–308.

71 Sabiston, C. M., McDonough, M. H., & Crocker, P. R. (2007), 'Psychosocial experiences of breast cancer survivors involved in a dragon boat program: Exploring links to positive psychological growth', *Journal of Sport and Exercise Psychology*, 29(4), p. 419; Brunet, J., McDonough, M. H., Hadd, V., Crocker, P. R., & Sabiston, C. M. (2010), 'The posttraumatic growth inventory: An examination of the factor structure and invariance among breast cancer survivors', *Psycho-Oncology*, 19(8), pp. 830–838; and Robinson, K. M., Piacentine, L. B., Waltke, L. J., Ng, A. V., & Tjoe, J. A. (2016), 'Survivors speak: A qualitative analysis of motivational factors influencing breast cancer survivors' participation in a sprint distance triathlon', *Journal of Clinical Nursing*, 25(1–2), pp. 247–256.

72 Vealey, R. S., & Perritt, N. C. (2015), 'Hardiness and optimism as predictors of the frequency of flow in collegiate athletes', *Journal of Sport Behavior*, 38(3), p. 321.

73 Mello, Z. R., Finan, L. J., & Worrell, F. C. (2013), 'Introducing an instrument to assess time orientation and time relation in adolescents', *Journal of Adolescence*, 36(3), pp. 551–563.

74 Significant work has been inspired by the work of Philip Zimbardo, who was in turned inspired by Thomas Cottle back in the 1960s. Zimbardo argues for what he calls a Balanced Time Perspective, which closely matches his personal relationship with the past, present and future. My view is that a present-future focus with a working knowledge of how they are connected is best for guiding action now that can shape a better future. This is different to Zimbardo's conclusion, and closer to the arguments of Cottle and, more recently, Zena Mello, a psychologist over at San Francisco State University. All of these researchers have shown that seeing the various time zones as connected, tipped towards the future, has benefits for academic and career performance, and well-being.

Further reading includes: Zimbardo, P. G., & Boyd, J. N. (2015), 'Putting time in perspective: A valid, reliable individual-differences metric', in *Time Perspective Theory; Review, Research and Application* (Springer International Publishing), pp. 17–55; Cottle, T. J. (1976), *Perceiving time: A Psychological Investigation with Men and Women* (John Wiley & Sons Inc); and Hammond, C. (2012), *Time Warped: Unlocking the Mysteries of Time Perception* (Canongate), which gives an engaging account of many aspects of time and how it changes our perception.

75 Functional helplessness.

76 Wadey, R., Evans, L., Hanton, S., & Neil, R. (2012), 'An examination of hardiness throughout the sport-injury process: A qualitative follow-up study', *British Journal of Health Psychology*, 17(4), pp. 872–893.

77 Salim, J., Wadey, R., & Diss, C. (2015), 'Examining the relationship between hardiness and perceived stress-related growth in a sport injury context', *Psychology of Sport and Exercise*, 19, pp. 10–17.

78 Sarkar, M., Fletcher, D., & Brown, D. J. (2015), 'What doesn't kill me . . . Adversity-related experiences are vital in the development of superior Olympic performance', *Journal of Science and Medicine in Sport*, 18(4), pp. 475–479.

79 Jostmann, N. B., & Koole, S. L. (2010), 'Dealing with high demands: The role of action versus state orientation', *Handbook of Personality and Self-regulation*, 14, pp. 332–352 and Koole, S. L., & Jostmann, N. B. (2004), 'Getting a grip on your feelings: Effects of action orientation and external demands on intuitive affect regulation', *Journal of Personality and Social Psychology*, 87(6), p. 974.

80 Koole, S. L., Jostmann, N. B., & Baumann, N. (2012), 'Do demanding conditions help or hurt self regulation?' *Social and Personality Psychology Compass*, 6(4), pp 328–346.

81 Mongrain, M., Komeylian, Z., & Barnhart, R. (2016), 'Happiness vs. mindfulness exercises for individuals vulnerable to depression', *The Journal of Positive Psychology*, 11(4), 2016, pp. 366–377.

Chapter 6: Three Streams of #Now

82 D'Argembeau, A., Renaud, O., & Van der Linden, M. (2011), 'Frequency, characteristics and functions of future-oriented thoughts in daily life', *Applied Cognitive Psychology*, 25(1), pp. 96–103; and Barsics, C., Van der Linden, M., & D'Argembeau, A. (2015), 'Frequency, characteristics, and perceived functions of emotional future thinking in daily life', *The Quarterly Journal of Experimental Psychology*, pp. 1–17.

83 Norman, C. C., & Aron, A. (2003), 'Aspects of possible self that predict motivation to achieve or avoid it', *Journal of Experimental Social Psychology*, 39 (5), pp. 500–507, Lewis, N. A., & Oyserman, D. (2015), 'When does the future begin? Time metrics matter, connecting present and future selves', *Psychological Science*, pp. 1–10, and Oyserman, D., Destin, M., & Novin, S. (2015), 'The context-sensitive future self: Possible selves motivate in context, not otherwise', *Self and Identity*, 14(2), pp. 173–188.

84 Oberauer, K., Farrell, S., Jarrold, C., & Lewandowsky, S. (2016), 'What limits working memory capacity?' *Psychological Bulletin* advance online publication; Cowan, N. (2010), 'The magical mystery tour: How is working memory capacity limited, and why?' *Current Directions in Psychological Science*, 19(1), pp. 51–57; and Jostmann, N. B., & Koole, S. L. (2006), 'On the waxing and waning of working memory: Action orientation moderates the impact of demanding relationship primes on working memory capacity', *Personality and Social Psychology Bulletin*, 32(12), pp. 1,716–1,728.

85 Kruglanski, A. W., Chernikova, M., Babush, M., Dugas, M., & Schumpe, B. (2015), 'The architecture of goal systems: Multifinality, equifinality, and counterfinality in means–end relations', *Advances in Motivation Science*, 2, pp. 69–98.

86 Sanbonmatsu, D. M., Strayer, D. L., Medeiros-Ward, N., & Watson, J. M. (2013), 'Who multi-tasks and why? Multi-tasking ability, perceived multi-tasking ability, impulsivity, and sensation seeking', *Public Library of Science*, 8(1), e54402. Doi:10.1.1371/journal.pone.0054402.

87 Medeiros-Ward, N., Watson, J. M., & Strayer, D. L. (2015), 'On supertaskers and the neural basis of efficient multitasking', *Psychonomic Bulletin & Review*, 22(3), pp. 876–883.

88 Baethge, A., & Rigotti, T. (2013), 'Interruptions to workflow: Their relationship with irritation and satisfaction with performance, and the mediating roles of time pressure and mental demands', *Work & Stress*, 27(1), pp. 43–63.

89 For example: De la Croix, D., & Licandro, O. (2015), 'The longevity of

famous people from Hammurabi to Einstein', *Journal of Economic Growth*, 20(3), pp. 263–303; Palacios, T., Solari, C., & Bains, W. (2015), 'Prosper and live long: Productive life span tracks increasing overall life span over historical time among privileged worker groups', *Rejuvenation Research*, 18(3), pp. 234–244; Guven, C., & Saloumidis, R. (2014), 'Life satisfaction and longevity: longitudinal evidence from the german socio-economic panel', *German Economic Review*, 15(4), pp. 453–472; 'Zhang, Y., & Han, B. (2016), 'Positive affect and mortality risk in older adults: A meta-analysis', *PsyCh Journal*. doi: 10.1002/pchj.129.

90 Franklin, M. S., Mrazek, M. D., Anderson, C. L., Smallwood, J., Kingstone, A., & Schooler, J. W. (2013), 'The silver lining of a mind in the clouds: Interesting musings are associated with positive mood while mind-wandering', *Frontiers in Psychology*, 4, published 27 August 2013. doi: 10.3389/fpsyg.2013.00583.

91 Oettingen, G., Mayer, D., & Portnow, S. (2016), 'Pleasure now, pain later: Positive fantasies about the future predict symptoms of depression', *Psychological Science*, 0956797615620783.

Toolkit 4: Breathing Deeply, Moving Forward

92 Gillen, J. B., Martin, B. J., MacInnis, M. J., Skelly, L. E., Tarnopolsky, M. A., & Gibala, M. J. (2016), 'Twelve weeks of sprint interval training improves indices of cardiometabolic health similar to traditional endurance training despite a five-fold lower exercise volume and time commitment', *PloS one*, 11(4), e0154075.

93 Mehta, R. K., Shortz, A. E., & Benden, M. E. (2015), 'Standing up for learning: A pilot investigation on the neurocognitive benefits of stand-biased school desks'. *International Journal of Environmental Research and Public Health*, 13(1), p. 59.

94 Pascoe, M. C., & Bauer, I. E. (2015), 'A systematic review of randomised control trials on the effects of yoga on stress measures and mood', *Journal of Psychiatric Research*, 68, pp. 270–282.

95 Dehghan, M. (2016), 'Review on theorizing yoga and dance/movement therapy as a Mindfulness Skill', *The International Journal of Indian Psychology*, Volume 3, Issue 2, No.8, DIP: 18.01.151/20160302 I, (Chicago).

96 Tolnai, N., Szabó, Z., Köteles, F., & Szabo, A. (2016), 'Physical and psychological benefits of once-a-week pilates exercises in young sedentary women: A 10-week longitudinal study', *Physiology & Behavior*, 63, pp. 211–218.

97 One version of the exercise is included on the DVD in Williams, M., & Penman, D. (2011). *Mindfulness: A practical guide to finding peace in a frantic world*, Hachette UK.

98 Creswell, J. D., & Lindsay, E. K. (2014), 'How does mindfulness training affect health? A mindfulness stress buffering account', *Current Directions in Psychological Science*, 23(6), pp. 401–407.

ACKNOWLEDGEMENTS

Many people helped in making this book possible. They made the arguments in this book stronger and supported me when I needed to keep moving.

There are the Nowists in my life who have given me living examples that have given birth to ideas shared in this book. They are rarely still, always moving, never defeated. Some of them are so extraordinary that they have not been included in this book because they might have been found too unbelievable, yet they are real, ordinary, and amazing. We all know at least one force of nature.

Several of the psychologists and scientists whose work is discussed in this book helped with their time and comments while I was writing it. These include Arie Kruglanski, Stephen Joseph, Jocelyn Bélanger, Valerie Reyna, Adam Galinsky, Meghan McDonough, Ed Stupple, Terry Connolly, Jason McIntyre, David Strayer, Jonathan Schooler, Carl Honoré, Gary Klein and Philip Tetlock, whose work on super-forecasting led to a discussion about the existence for super-fast, super-forecasters, who can make rapid micro adjustments to forecasts to help them move at speed. And thanks to everyone else who has done insightful work that adds to human knowledge about how we regulate emotion and keep moving.

Several drafts were read in detail by my remarkable daughter Brontë, while she task-juggled with her psychology work at York University, England, and still stretched time to provide cheerleading and knowledgeable feedback. She also reached out to her extended #Now, showing material to friends, Will Strawson, Niall Kirkham, Ross Johnson, Ben Pickard, Andy Whyte, who gave their opinions on posters and diagrams.

The drafts were also read by my super-cool, super-talented son Zak, who also provided feedback. Particularly on word choice, and graphical choices – and he did it in-between coursework and heading off to Copenhagen for the summer. Reuben, my eldest son, modelled the calmness of a functional impulsive. While my youngest son, provided daily commentary as we walked together to school each morning and in situations in which the ideas might prove useful. And, if needed, we would encourage each other to 'have an amazing day, and if you can't, survive it!' so that we could get unstuck and embrace the joy of moving forward.

And thanks to my family, friends and clients, who helpfully let me share ideas from the book and then put them to work in their daily lives. My goal was to describe the Nowist mindset well enough to inspire me, my loved ones and others who could choose to adopt some of their perspectives and behaviours. They tell me the ideas work for them. The Nowist concepts have undoubtedly helped me get started and keep rolling even in very demanding situations.

And to my Editor, Lucy Warburton, who passionately believes in the idea that life is best lived forwards. She found my writing, tracked me down to France and convinced me to write this book. Her conviction required coaxing and persuasion over many months, so that I would find ways of creating space to write and research. It also involved her ingenious organising strategy, perhaps rarely seen in publishing. Each part of the process, from editing, copy-editing via Josh Ireland, proof-reading, to type-setting, moving along with my writing. And her calm insistence that 'it would be great if you could send me x by tomorrow morning' a delightfully effective way of inspiring my inner Nowist.

I also appreciate the innovations and evolution that allowed this book to be written while moving, in taxis, stations, airports and beaches, on my feet, with my thumbs, on mobile Word, and an iPhone.

And, despite protests that acknowledgements are not wanted, it seems wise to mention my wisest critic and fiercest supporter. As you wish.